The Smugg
and other stories

By the same authors

The Tufton Hill Lot
(6 plays to read or record)

The Smuggler

and other stories

Paul Groves
Head of English,
St Hugh's Church of England Comprehensive School,
Grantham

Nigel Grimshaw
Formerly Senior Lecturer in English,
Kesteven College of Education,
Peterborough

John Murray

First published 1981
Reprinted 1984

Typeset by Inforum Ltd, Portsmouth

Printed in Hong Kong by
Wing King TongCo Ltd

British Library Cataloguing in Publication Data

Groves, Paul
The smuggler and other stories.
1. Readers – 1950 –
I. Title II. Grimshaw, Nigel
428.6

ISBN 0-7195-3867-X

Contents

The Contents

The Smuggler

The wide plain was dry and dusty, baked in the sun. By the river that marked the border between the two countries, stood a customs post. A rough track led down the hill to it and beyond the post this track became a good road across the plain.

The Chief Customs Inspector stood outside the customs house. He was looking up the hill. A figure leading a donkey was coming down. The Inspector nodded to himself and went inside the building.

'You two!' he ordered. 'A man is about to cross the border. Stop him and search him well.'

'Yes, sir!' The two lounging guards buckled on their pistols and went outside. The Inspector followed. They all watched the approaching figure. When they could see it clearly, the two men looked at each other and then at the Inspector. They seemed puzzled but they said nothing.

The man coming down the track was old. His hat, as dusty and old as its owner, was shapeless. His shirt was grey with use and washing. It was torn at the shoulder and had a blue patch on each elbow. His trousers were worn at the knee and his boots were tied with string. His plodding donkey had seen better days. When the guards stopped them, it stood patiently with hanging head.

The two guards looked again at the Inspector.

'Go on!' he commanded. 'Search him!'

They shrugged and started the search. The donkey

had two sacks on its back. They lifted these down and opened them. They contained small, greenish, sour-looking oranges.

'Tip them out,' ordered the Inspector. 'Examine them.'

They did. They looked carefully at every orange until the sacks were empty.

'Now search him. And take his hat off. See that there is nothing inside it.'

They took off his hat and, when the Inspector ordered it, they took off the man's boots. He was hiding nothing. The goatskin in which he carried his water was also closely inspected. The Inspector even rapped his knuckles on the bucket slung on the donkey's back. In the silence the bucket made a dull, hollow clang.

When he had finished it was the old man's turn to look inquiringly and to hold up the bucket.

'A drink of water for the donkey?' he asked mildly.

'Oh, go on, go on!' snarled the Inspector. The old man went down to the river and filled the bucket. When he came back the weight of it pulled him to one side. One of the customs officers made a movement. He would have gone to help the old man but the Inspector stopped him irritably. While the donkey drank he walked round it, tapping his shiny shoes with his cane.

'So, you're not smuggling anything today, eh, Paco?' he growled.

'No, your Excellency.'

'Tomorrow, maybe.'

'Not tomorrow, your Excellency.'

'We shall search you, anyway.'

'That is your duty, your Excellency.'

The Inspector sniffed. 'Paco,' he said. 'I know you of old. Once a smuggler, always a smuggler. You're still up to your old tricks.'

'I have been a smuggler,' said the old man, called Paco. 'I must admit it. But that was when I was young and foolish and greedy. With age comes wisdom. I know better now.'

'Paco – you're a rascal!' said the Inspector.

'We are all sinners, your Excellency,' said Paco.

'Oh! Get off with you. Go on! On your way!' the Inspector snapped.

The customs post for Parantina, the neighbouring country, was on the other side of the river. The old man stopped. A Parantinian customs official came out, looked at him and waved him on.

The old man went slowly along the road across the plain. The Inspector stood in the hot sun to watch him until he was almost out of sight. He had a frown on his face.

That evening the old man came back with his donkey. His sack was empty. The Inspector watched him again as he gave his donkey a drink from the river and filled his goatskin with water. As the old man began to toil homewards up the steep mountain track, the Inspector went back inside the customs post. His expression was fixed and determined.

The next morning the old man arrived at the customs post again with his donkey and the search was more thorough. This time they examined the sack and when they found that all it contained was inferior oranges, they combed the donkey. All they got from its hide was a lot of dust and a good many fleas. The Inspector did not say much to Paco and what he did say was sharp and angry. But they found nothing and they had to let the old man go.

Every day the old man would go to market in Parantina in the morning and return at evening. He never varied. He would stand patiently, like his donkey, to be searched and then, after he had given the donkey a drink, he would move on. In the evening he would return, water the donkey again, fill his goatskin and go home.

Every day, the Inspector grew more short-tempered. They continued to comb the donkey. The two customs officials would scratch themselves in bed at night and curse the donkey's fleas and the Inspector. They examined the old man's boots. Then they made him take off his trousers and shirt while the Inspector ran his finger along their seams to see that nothing had been hidden there. One day, in a rage, the Inspector made them cut all Paco's oranges in half. Paco took it all calmly. He still went on into Parantina. He said he could sell the oranges to a fruit juice factory and cut some of his losses. If he took them home again, they would only rot.

They examined the donkey's hooves, they looked in its mouth and up its nose. In desperation, the Inspector ordered them to look through the old man's hair and in his ears. Every day the search took longer – combing the donkey, examining it, squeezing the oranges (they never cut them open again after that first time), examining the old man, his boots and his clothes, turning his hat inside out. Just before the really hot weather started, the search was taking nearly an hour. Paco took it all in his stride. He even began to arrive an hour early at the customs post so that they could take as long as they liked over the search and still leave him enough time to get to the market in Parantina.

One day, when the orange season was almost over, Paco went down to the river with his bucket as usual. While he was getting water for the donkey, the Inspector came up to him and smiled. Paco smiled back.

'We have known each other for a long time, eh, Paco?' asked the Inspector.

'We have, your Excellency,' said Paco.

'You will not be coming this way next week, will you?'

'Today is my last day, your Excellency,' Paco told him. 'The oranges are finished.'

'Oh?' The Inspector's smile faded. 'The last day, eh?' Then he said. 'How long have we been searching you?'

'For more than a month,' said Paco.

'And we have found nothing.'

'There was nothing to find, your Excellency.'

'Listen, Paco.' The Inspector took the old man's sleeve in a friendly way. 'I'll make you an offer. Tell me what you've been smuggling and I won't do a thing about it.'

'Smuggling?' said Paco and he sounded hurt. 'I have not been smuggling, your Excellency.'

The Inspector took out his wallet and showed Paco enough money to pay for two days' oranges. 'Tell me, Paco,' he said, 'and these notes are yours.'

'I cannot take money dishonestly, your Excellency.' Paco shook his head. 'I have smuggled nothing.'

The Inspector gave him a long, angry stare. Then he growled in his throat, turned on his heel and let Paco give his donkey a drink and go on to the market. Paco did not come that way again.

That summer, the Inspector took his holiday in Parantina. One evening he was having a drink in a restaurant. Suddenly his glass stopped half way to his lips. He stared. Was that man Paco?

He was wearing a very expensive suit. He looked younger. He had with him a very pretty, dark-haired woman. Then he stood up to go and the Inspector saw that it was indeed Paco. He hurried across the restaurant and caught Paco up in the street outside. Paco and the girl with him were just about to get into a large, shining car with a smart-looking driver.

'Inspector!' said Paco. 'How nice to see an old friend.'

'Paco – ' the Inspector began, but Paco held up his hand.

'I'm sorry I can't stop,' he apologised. 'Carlotta and I are just driving to the airport. We're flying to Switzerland tonight. I have enough money there in the bank for us to live comfortably. We shan't be coming back.' He was going to get into the car. The Inspector stopped him.

'Paco!' he pleaded. 'Money in a Swiss bank? You *were* smuggling. Nothing will happen to you, I promise. But I shall not sleep at nights unless I know. What were you smuggling during those long weeks?'

'Gold,' said Paco. He got into the car and it drove off, leaving the Inspector frowning on the pavement.

Gold? He thought about it. Gold is precious but Paco must have smuggled a lot to make himself rich. How? Then his mind began to work and anger started to swell in him like a balloon. The gold would come illegally from the mine in the hills. Yes. But – ah! Gold is a metal. It can be beaten out into sheets. The sheets can be soldered or welded to make a bucket. The bucket can be kicked or banged and made to look old. Spray it with silver paint and coat it with dirt and you had – the old man's bucket. At the market you buy a real bucket and on the way home you kick it along the road until it, too, looks old.

His rage grew. But he had given his promise to Paco and he was a man of his word. He was also a wise man. He mastered his rage and sighed.

'Buckets!' he said.

'I beg your pardon, sir?' The doorman of the restaurant looked puzzled.

'He was smuggling buckets,' said the Inspector, striking himself on the forehead with his flat hand. He cursed and threw his arms up in the air. Then he let them fall, shrugged and went back into the restaurant.

'Buckets?' the doorman asked the empty air.

THE STORY

1 At the beginning of the story, why does the Inspector nod to himself before he goes inside the building?
2 Why were the two guards puzzled by the Inspector's order to search the man?
3 Why was the Inspector angry when the search was over?
4 Why, in time, did the customs officials come to curse the Inspector?
5 How do you think Paco felt every time each search was over? Why did he feel like that?
6 In which country could this story have taken place? What facts in the story helped you with the answer?
7 The Inspector offers Paco money for the secret of what he has been smuggling. Would you have taken the money and told the Inspector? Give reasons for your reply.

8 Why did Paco look younger when the Inspector saw him in the restaurant?

9 Whose side are you on in this story, Paco's or the Inspector's? Why?

YOUR OWN WRITING

1 The Inspector had obviously met Paco before. Had Paco tricked him then, too? Or had the Inspector caught Paco that time? What had Paco been smuggling then? Write the story.

2 What would you do if you had a lot of money? List some of the things you would buy. Would you spend it all on yourself?

3 The Inspector talks to a friend about Paco. Is the Inspector angry and does the friend laugh? Or is it the other way about? Does the friend suggest a way of catching Paco? Write the conversation out in the form of a short play.

Mrs Nightrider's Revenge

You keep glancing at me, young man. Do I seem a bit strange? And are you thinking it's a long way to the next station? And that there are just the two of us alone together in this compartment?

Don't be afraid. I only get really fierce with people who annoy me – like Mr Nibbs. You remind me of him. That's why I was looking at you. I don't usually like travelling by train. It's too noisy for an old woman like me. So a nice little chat like this helps to pass the time.

Like you, Mr Nibbs was a quiet, grey sort of person. He had the same sad, puzzled look in his eyes the first time I saw him, too. He works for the Council – in the offices – and he's never late. And yet he's a man with a secret. He goes off somewhere every Saturday afternoon and he doesn't tell his wife about it.

His eyes are still sad. They're like that because there's something inside Mr Nibbs that yearns to get out. I didn't know that when I first met him. Neither did he.

It all began when Mr Clumber called Mr Nibbs into his office. Mr Clumber is his boss.

'Ah! There you are, Nibbs,' he said, holding out an official file. 'Deal with this, will you?'

'Yes, sir,' said Nibbs, taking the file.

'We're planning a new development up at Mirkwood,' Clumber told him. 'Everything's ready to move in about six months time.'

'Yes, sir,' said Nibbs.

'Just one snag,' Clumber went on. 'There's a cottage right in the middle of the site. We wrote to the tenant but we got no reply. One of the officials went up. All he got was abuse. He handled it badly, no doubt. I rely on you to do better.'

'Yes, sir,' said Nibbs.

'It's all in the file,' Clumber said. 'Read it through. Any questions – come to me. Otherwise – slip up there today. Deal with the matter. Use tact. But we want that cottage empty. Understand?'

'Yes, sir,' said Nibbs.

He read the file. It was all quite clear. Mrs Nightrider had no right to the cottage. He had no questions for Mr Clumber. So he went out to Mirkwood.

It was right at the end of the bus route. He was the last passenger. The bus turned round and went back to town. Mr Nibbs, left alone, looked about him.

He could see why the place was called Mirkwood. A clump of trees grew close to the road. Even in daylight, they looked dark and mysterious. They would have to come down when the new development started.

The cottage was not welcoming either. Its thatched roof came down low like frowning eyebrows. Its garden was overgrown and its windows stared at him like hard, mad eyes. But Mr Nibbs polished up his smile and knocked at the door.

It took a long time to open. The woman who opened it was elderly and oddly dressed. She reminded him of a witch.

She glared at Mr Nibbs. 'What do you want?' she snapped.

'I'm from the Council, madam,' he said gently.

'Are you?' she snapped even more fiercely. 'Well – I warned you what would happen if another of you hounds came snuffling round here!'

'Please!' he said. 'We want to offer you another house. May I come in?'

'No!' she replied.

'Then let me explain,' he said smoothly. He tried to paint a bright picture of the new house she would have. But he told her that she would have to leave the cottage.

'Threats!' she said, so fiercely that he stepped back. 'Coming here growling and snapping and barking at a poor old lady! You're curs, the lot of you! Mongrels! Hounds!' She stopped and then she slowly smiled a frightening smile. 'That's it! Yes!' she hissed. 'Dog by nature – dog you shall be!'

She flicked her fingers at him, muttering, and a sudden dizziness came over him. He was dazzled by a painful light and he felt himself shrinking.

When he came to, he was staring at the footworn doorstep and the slam of the door resounded in his ears.

And that was not all of it. He looked at his hands and they were paws. It took more than a minute for it to sink in. But he realised at last. Mrs Nightrider had reminded him of a witch because she was a witch. And she had turned him into a dog.

He was filled with horror and despair. 'Please!' he wanted to say. He tried to knock at the door. But the 'please' came out as a small, sad whine and his claws only scratched feebly on the wood. For a moment or two he stood there whimpering before he went slowly down the path. It was no use turning to Mrs Nightrider for help. But what could he say to Mr Clumber? He would most certainly lose his job. Dogs couldn't work in offices. And what would his wife say? She hated dogs. She thought that they were messy, untidy, dirty things. Mr Nibbs could have wept.

It was then that he caught sight of the prowling cat. And a force beyond himself took over. He barked. It was a powerful, challenging sound. He ran like the wind. The cat fled and finally scrambled in terror up a tree.

Mr Nibbs stood below panting, giving loud, excited barks. And a very strange thing happened. He began to feel marvellous.

His sight, as a dog, wasn't as good as it had been as a man. He seemed to see things in black and white and not in colour. But his sense of smell! He inhaled whole symphonies of delicious odours.

His wife fed Mr Nibbs on puddings and pies. Though neat, he was tubby and a bit short of breath when he hurried. But this new doggy Mr Nibbs was strong and slim and swift. And he was free!

His mother had been strict with young Cedric Nibbs. Then he had married a woman who had an equally firm hand. Both Mrs Nibbses disapproved of many things like dashing about and noise and singing and laughter. They had made Mr Nibbs a neat man. They and the years had made him grey. And yet – all the time – inside neat, grey Mr Nibbs a second self had been lurking. A daring, swift, heroic self! And Mrs Nightrider had set it free. Mr Nibbs took full advantage of his freedom.

He started slowly. He barked and swore at the cat. The cat spat and swore back. But that got boring. And Mr Nibbs had become aware of a fine perfume. It came from something dead in a field. Mr Nibbs found it and had a good roll in the splendid smell so that he could take it with him wherever he went.

He chased a rabbit. It got away but he frightened the life out of it. He had a drink from a puddle. The muddy water tasted like wine. He ambled along a lane, sniffing delightedly at the smell of himself and all the other interesting smells around him. He had a bit of a dig into a rat hole. Later it was difficult to remember all the excitements. There were so many of them.

He met Sam. Sam was a biggish dog of no particular breed with flopping ears. They made a good team. Together they went for an old man on a bike. He yelled at them and cursed them and tried to kick out at them with one leg so that he nearly fell off his bike. They dashed away, roaring with evil, doggish laughter. They ravaged several back gardens. Mr Nibbs had to make a frantic, scrambling leap over a back fence to escape a woman with a sweeping brush. It was wonderful.

The climax came with a raid on the butcher's. Sam said it couldn't be done. All the meat would be safely under glass. Mr Nibbs, feeling peckish, insisted. They nearly grabbed a pound of steak that the butcher was weighing out but he was after them too quickly with his chopping knife, and all the customers cried out and swung shopping bags. They got away quite easily.

In the escape, though, Mr Nibbs was separated from Sam. He went like the wind down a side street, his spirits soaring. He felt godlike. But then came tragedy.

He had stopped on a corner to get his breath and to

look around for Sam. It was late afternoon and the street was empty. Without warning, the dizziness returned and the world changed.

This time, when he came back to himself, he didn't need to look. He had hands. He wore a neat, grey suit. He was taller. He was the old Mr Nibbs again. He felt numbed with the shock of it. He couldn't believe that fate could be so unkind. Like a sleepwalker, he went back to the office and reported to Mr Clumber. He hardly noticed Mr Clumber's response. Later he went home and talked to his wife. No one said anything. Evidently in other people's eyes there had been no change in him. Outwardly he was still just the same old neat grey Mr Nibbs. But inwardly he was different. Inwardly he yearned for the excitement of that afternoon.

Why did he want to be a dog again? Why couldn't he use his imagination? Ah! In Mr Nibbs's neat grey mind all the imagination had died. That was why he wanted to see Mrs Nightrider again. He needed her desperately. That was why he had to go back to Mirkwood. He would plead with her. He would make her turn him into a dog again.

He told no one about it. How could he? They would think that he had gone mad. And he couldn't go to Mirkwood that evening or any other evening that week. Mrs Nibbs always had too much for him to do. But on Saturdays she let him go out for a walk by himself in the afternoons. So the very next Saturday, trembling with anticipation, he went up to Mirkwood and the cottage.

And that's the joke of it! Mrs Nightrider had gone!

She'd gone for good. She was a sly old thing. She'd seen how things stood and she'd left. She knew they'd be back again to harass her and she didn't need the cottage. Nor did she want a new house from the Council. She's got more interesting places to visit. That's what she's been doing all these weeks by day and by night. By night she rides the sky. But by day she travels just like anyone else.

How do I know all this? That's a silly question. I have ways. For me, you see, it's easy. I can find out all sorts of things about all sorts of people. I know that Mr Nibbs has been back to that cottage Saturday after Saturday. But he won't ever see Mrs Nightrider again. How do I know? Isn't it obvious?

How this train does rattle along! And isn't it a long way to the next station!

THE STORY

1 What is your opinion of Mr Clumber? Do you think he was a good man or a bad man to work for? Say why you think so.
2 How did Mr Nibbs feel about Mrs Nightrider when he first met her?
3 How can you tell that he felt a bit uneasy even before he met her?
4 Just after Mr Nibbs found out that he was a dog, was he thinking sensibly or not? Give some reasons for your answer.
5 What is your opinion of Mrs Nibbs and Mr Nibbs's mother? Had they treated him well or badly? Why do you think so?
6 Is there anything about Mr Nibbs's life as a dog that you

would find unpleasant? What? What would you enjoy most about it?

7 How do you know that Mr Nibbs was always very obedient to his wife?
8 How did Mrs Nightrider know everything about Mr Nibbs?
9 How do you think the young man in the compartment with her felt?

YOUR OWN WRITING

1 The young man arrives safely at his station. He tells a friend about Mrs Nightrider. Does the friend think he is making it up? Does he say that Mrs Nightrider was simply telling lies to frighten the young man? Or does he believe the story? Does he want to find Mrs Nightrider to ask her to help him with something? Write your answers out in play form.
2 Do you like dogs? Make a list of all the different breeds you know.
3 Do you dislike dogs? Is there one particular dog you dislike? Make a list of the reasons for your dislike.
4 Mrs Nightrider would not dress like a witch while she went by train. But she did seem a bit strange. Describe what she looked like and the clothes she wore.

Bigger than the Beatles

The music thumped down the stairs.

'Turn that noise off!' yelled Mr Wilson, wiping a cornflake from the corner of his mouth.

'He can't hear you,' said Mrs Wilson. She looked tired and drawn.

'It's bad enough at night. But at breakfast as well! I won't have it.'

'I'll tell him to turn it down.'

'He'll go deaf. I read a report in the paper last week. Stone deaf before he's twenty.' He turned his anger on the egg in front of him, slicing off the top so viciously that the yolk ran down the shell.

'Jimmy! Jimmy! Can't you turn that down a bit? Your father's complaining.' She walked upstairs.

'Oh, Mum, it's no good if it's quiet. It's heavy rock.'

'Well, just wait till he's gone to work. You should be ready as well.'

'I'm not going in today.'

'Aren't you well?' she said anxiously, wiping a wisp of hair from her creased brow.

'No, I'm just not going in.'

'Please don't let your father hear about it.'

'I'll tell you later, Mum. I've got to meet Pete.'

She went slowly downstairs.

'I don't know what young people are coming to,' Mr Wilson went on. 'That music – if you can call it that! Those clothes! That hair! I suppose he'll want earrings next. A good dose of the strap some of them want. Do them good.'

She said nothing as she handed him his lunch tin and flask.

'May be in late. I've got a darts meeting when I finish at the works. Cheerio.'

'Aren't you going to kiss me?'

'Oh, yes.'

'You don't have to.'

'Sorry.' He gave her a peck on the cheek.

As soon as he had left Jimmy shot downstairs. 'Jimmy!' she called. But he had gone.

He had no bus fare so he walked round to Pete's. He felt cold even though he had his leather jacket on. He ran part of the way till his lungs ached. Pete answered the door. 'Save your breath for the big number, mate,' he said.

Larry was there already and so was Tyke. Pete played drums, Larry bass guitar. Jimmy played the guitar with Tyke and he did the vocals as well. Tyke was picking out a few chords. Then he went into 'Satisfaction', a great guitar solo.

Jimmy was anxious to join Tyke. He had been coming to Pete's for three months now since Pete first lent him a guitar. For the past month he had given up his job as an apprentice bricklayer so that he could practise with the group all day. He reckoned they would make it. They could be bigger than the Beatles. They had already done three gigs and a manager from London had said they could record their first demo tape in a month or two. He was giving them some financial backing.

'Told your family yet?' asked Pete.

'Telling me Mum this afternoon,' Jimmy said. 'It's been difficult not to let it out especially after that great last gig.'

'What about your Dad?'

'I'll tell him tonight. My mind's made up.'

But it was not that easy. He was just about to tell his mother when his father came in unexpectedly. 'They've cancelled the match,' he said.

'Is it so bad to have one evening at home?' she asked.

'Huh,' he grunted.

It was now or never, before they rowed. 'I'm in a pop group!' he blurted out.

'You what?' said his father.

'I'm going to be a super-star. Bigger than the Beatles.'

'That's nice,' said his Mum. She did not smile though and her lips were pressed together.

'You're playing that music? You don't know a note.'

'I'm learning at Pete's.'

'Oh, he comes into it, does he? It's a good thing you're not doing it here is all I can say.'

'I've given up my job as a brickie.'

'You've what?'

'I've given up my job.'

'Your apprenticeship?'

'Yeh.'

'To play that useless music?'

'I'm going to be a star. This bloke who's helping us says – '

'You must get it back at once!'

'I'm never going back, Dad.'

'Please, Jack.'

'You keep out of this. Get up to your room at once!'

'I'm seventeen.'

'Get up to your room. I'll sort you out.'

'Jack!'

He sat on the bed. He could hear them shouting at each other downstairs. Then his father came up. He braced himself for a beating. But his father came in slowly. 'Look, son,' he said. 'They come to no good, those people. They take drugs. They die young. Look at that Jimi Bendrix.'

'Hendrix,' said Jimmy.

'And that yobbo, Vicious. Even Presley. It's no good, son.'

'My mind's made up, Dad.' He waited for the first blow. But his father just bellowed. 'Right! You can get out of my house then. You're no son of mine. I don't want to know you. First thing in the morning – out!'

He listened to another row downstairs as he slowly started to pack. Then his mother came up.

'You see, it's now or never, Mum. We've got this bloke who'll manage us. He liked our gig.'

She went and looked out of the window.

'Please, Mum. Trust me.'

When she turned again her face was moist with tear streaks.

'I don't want you to leave home, Jimmy.'

'He says I've got to go.'

'Not yet, Jimmy.'

'There's no other way.'

'Please, Jimmy, give up this idea and go and get your job back for my sake.'

'This chance means everything to me.'

She sat down. 'All right. I didn't want to tell you this. I didn't want to tell anyone. I'm not well.'

'You're often not well, Mum.'

'This time I'm really not well. I've been to see the doctor. He's given me a year, Jimmy.'

A hand of ice gripped his heart.

'There. I wasn't going to tell you.'

'How can he be sure?'

'I've been to the hospital.' She fell into his arms.

'Aw, Mum. Is that why Dad's so bad-tempered?'

'I haven't told him, Jimmy. I don't want him to know yet.'

'You must, Mum.'

'Things haven't been right between us for years. You must have guessed. I'll tell him at the right time.'

'You must tell him now, Mum.'

'No!'

He hugged her tightly. She felt so frail. Why had he not guessed? He had been so taken up with his music.

'I'd like a year with no fuss. You mean so much to me. When I've gone you can do what you like.'

He could say nothing now. No words would come. It was as though he had fallen into a great pit. He would never have this chance again. They would get someone else. 'Oh, Mum.' He ran downstairs.

He found himself running up the hill out of town. It was dark. He blundered into someone but he did not stop. He just ran on and on. On the brow he finally clung to the railings above the works and looked down on the town. There was a row of lights by the station in the distance. As a child he had called these the lights of the future. He saw them lighting his way out of the town to stardom. But what now? He could not leave his mother now.

A policeman came up. 'What's up, son?' he asked.

'Nothing,' said Jimmy.

'It can't be nothing.'

He gripped the railings harder. 'No, it's nothing,' he said.

'It must be something.'

'My Mum's going to die,' he said.

'That's bad, son.'

'And I was going to be bigger than the Beatles.'

'Come and have a cup of tea, son.'

In a steamed-up café he was surprised to find himself pouring out his heart to this total stranger. The policeman listened. 'If you go back and help your Mum,' he said, 'you *will* be bigger than the Beatles.'

'How can I be?' asked Jimmy.

'They didn't have to make this kind of sacrifice,' the policeman said. 'Drink up your tea. Think about it. It was much easier for them. Nothing as hard as what you've got to do.'

He twirled his spoon in the cup. 'Yeh,' he said. 'Yeh.'

THE STORY

1 What is Mr Wilson's opinion of pop music?
2 Why do teenagers like such loud music?
3 What early indications are there that Mrs Wilson is not well?
4 How would you describe the character of Mr Wilson?
5 Should Mr Wilson have mentioned Hendrix, Vicious and Presley? Is it a fair sample of what happens to pop musicians?
6 In what state is the marriage of Mr and Mrs Wilson?
7 Should Mrs Wilson have told Jimmy about her illness or not? Give your reasons.

8 What are the chances of succeeding in the pop world?
9 What group would you most like to be a member of?
10 What do you think of Jimmy's decision at the end of the story?

YOUR OWN WRITING

1 Describe a disco. Make it full of colour.
2 Write about the relationship between yourself and your parents, or about an imaginary conflict between parents and a son or daughter.
3 Jimmy makes the opposite decision and tells his mother. Write out their conversation in play form.
4 What are the current top ten in the charts? Make a list.

That's Show Business

She had time for a cup of tea before the train went. She pushed open the door of the buffet room and went in. The usual early morning commuters were inside. She knew many of them by sight but not by name. She got a cup of tea and sat down to look at the paper.

Once when she glanced over the top of it she saw a new face. It belonged to a young man in jeans with a shock of blond hair. He was certainly good-looking and he smiled at her as she looked over her paper. It was such an engaging smile that before she realised it she had smiled back. She quickly looked down again at her paper. But she was conscious that someone had come over and had sat down at her table and she thought it was him.

It was. He sat there and coughed several times. 'Excuse me,' he said. 'Can you help me out?'

She went red. 'How can I do that?' she asked.

'I need a girl,' he said.

He certainly was the fastest worker she had ever met. 'Many men do,' she said, 'but they don't go about it in such a cheeky way.'

'No,' he said. 'You've got me wrong. I'm in great need of a girl.'

'I have a train to catch,' she said, getting up quickly.

'Let me finish, please. I'm in great need of a girl for my act. I'm in show business.'

She gave a nervous laugh. 'Oh,' she said. 'I have a job

and a train to catch.'

'No, please listen. Catch the next one.'

Something about him made her sit down again. There was another train in ten minutes.

'I do a variety act – a bit of juggling, fire-eating and things. It's a great act. I'm appearing tonight at the After Eight Club.'

'Congratulations.'

'I need a girl like you.'

'I've never done anything like that in my life.'

'You don't need any experience. You have the looks and the figure for it. You're tall and dark-haired. You have a bit of a Red Indian look about you. It could fit my act.'

'No one's ever said that to me before.' She laughed, though.

'You look even better when you laugh,' he said. 'You've got lovely teeth.'

'Flattery will get you nowhere.'

'It's not flattery. It's the truth. You're just the girl I need.'

'What about my job? I can't just not go.'

'Telephone them,' he said. 'Say you're sick. Just for one day, please.'

'I couldn't do that.'

'Well, say you have urgent business to attend to.'

'Yes, show business,' she retorted.

'I can't lose this booking. I'll get a bad name.'

'But my job!'

'I'll pay you more than you get, I bet.'

'I might work for a millionaire for all you know,' she said. But there was something in his manner that urged her to be foolish. 'What would I have to do?'

'Just throw a few juggling clubs to me, help with the

fire-eating, but most of all be your pretty self.'

'Fire-eating?'

'It's not dangerous.'

'This is ridiculous,' she said. 'I just don't believe it.'

'Say yes.'

'All right. I'll do it. I must be mad but I'll do it.'

'You darling,' he said. He leant across and kissed her on the cheek. 'Come on.'

He took her by the hand. His grip was powerful. She imagined every one of the regular commuters was staring at her and she was glad to get out of the buffet. On the platform she stopped. 'Look, I don't even know your name.'

'Great Chief Laughing Water,' he said, grinning.

'Your proper name.'

'Paul,' he said.

She thought it suited him. 'I'm Joanne.'

'I like that,' he said.

They went to a local church hall where he had permission to rehearse. She practised throwing juggling clubs to him and handling the fire-eating equipment. It was quite hard at first but eventually she got the hang of it. He was delighted. 'You'll be great!' he said. 'Much better than my last girl. Here's your costume. Try it on.'

'There's not much of it,' she said.

'We can't hide your prettiness in clothes,' he told her.

She went into the toilet and tried it on. It was as brief as a bikini and had sequins on it. There was a feathered head-dress as well. She came out into the hall feeling very self-conscious.

'It's a perfect fit,' he said. 'I knew you had the figure

for it. You darling!' He kissed her for the second time that day on the cheek. 'Come on, get back into your own clothes. I'm taking you out to lunch.'

They went into the best hotel in town where he bought her a delicious lunch: prawn cocktail, steak cooked in wine and cheesecake. He insisted that she shared a bottle of wine with him and she noticed that he filled her glass up more often than his own. She felt a little drunk by the time she had finished the meal.

'I don't feel quite so guilty about work,' she said.

'Good. That's my girl,' he said.

'What do we do now?'

'Just a bit more practice.'

'I thought we had done it all.'

'There's one more thing.'

'What's that?'

'The climax of the act.'

'What is it?'

'I'll show you, darling.' He had started to call her darling all the time now. Very theatrical, she thought.

During the morning she had noticed that they did not use one part of the equipment which was a big board. Now he set it up at the end of the room. Then he came up and gave her a little hug. 'Darling!' he said. 'Do you think you can stand prettily in front of this board?'

'What for?' she asked.

'Just while I throw a few knives at it.'

'You what?'

'Throw a few knives at it. I'm a knife-thrower as well as a juggler and fire-eater.'

She was angry.

'You've tricked me,' she said.

'Me?'

'The answer is no.'

'But, darling, there's nothing to it.'

'No.'

'It's so simple. That's why I left it to the end.'

'No.'

'You just stand in front of this board.'

'No.'

'Look. Watch me make a pattern of knives on the board.'

'Not with me there.'

'I can do it blindfolded.'

'No.'

'Just let me throw them on one side.'

'No, I'm going home.'

'But, darling, the show must go on. I must do the knife-throwing. It's in my contract. Please.' He went up to her, took her in his arms, and kissed her. Her opposition melted away.

'Well, all right,' she said. 'The whole day's a mad one. I suppose I've let myself in for it. But please leave plenty of space between me and the knives.'

'Of course, darling.'

After several goes she stopped flinching but she could not stop blinking. 'Never mind,' he said. 'It could help the act, if you looked a bit frightened. Come on, let's go for a walk.'

They walked by the river. It was sunny and the blossom was on the may trees. 'How do you come to be doing this act?' she asked.

'I was a commuter, like you. I had a steady job in a bank. But I felt like a rat in a cage behind those windows. I started off doing the act as an amateur and as it went well I took the plunge, gave up my job, and became a professional.'

They sat on a seat and watched the swans. He put his arm around her. 'I could grow quite fond of you,' he said. 'You're very nice as well as brave.'

'I thought this was a business arrangement,' she said. But he did not take his arm away.

'Of course,' he said. 'Can I kiss you?'

'You have twice already.'

'I mean properly.'

'You tricked me.'

'Well, let's kiss and make up.' He kissed her tenderly three times. 'Nice' he said. Then he leant back against the seat and went to sleep.

She was amazed and a little insulted. Then she thought: 'Now would be the time to go and leave him and his mad act.' She really was being stupid. She had a good job at the office. But he looked so handsome asleep. And there, on the seat by the river, with the swans gliding by, she knew that she loved him.

He woke after half an hour. 'I needed that, though it was a dangerous thing to do. You might have run away.'

'What, and ruin the act?' She laughed.

'You're a real professional,' he told her.

They went in his car to the After Eight Club. When she had changed into her costume she said, 'I'm beginning to have butterflies in my stomach.'

'That's good,' he said. 'All true artistes are nervous.' He kissed her. 'Just trust me,' he said.

The act passed like a dream. She loved the lights and

the applause from the audience. He was splendid. He was bare to the waist with a big head-dress of feathers. She could see that this act was his whole life. Surprisingly quickly they had reached the knife-throwing.

She went to stand in front of the board. As she walked her legs trembled. She pressed her back against the board. The band's music got loud then suddenly stopped. In the deep silence he raised his arm. The knife glinted. Then he started to throw.

The knives thudded round her arms. They were much closer than they had been at rehearsal. 'He's tricked me again,' she thought.

He smiled at her. Then he stopped throwing and came up. 'Will you marry me?' he whispered.

'No,' she said.

He went back to his place. He threw knives round her legs. Then he came forward again and whispered, 'Please marry me. I can't guarantee to throw straight unless you do.'

'No,' she whispered.

This time the knives thudded in round her head. She felt trapped by them.

He came up. 'I have one last knife to throw by your heart,' he said. 'Please say yes.'

She looked at him as he stood there under the powerful lights. She knew she loved everything about him. Her head was in a whirl. 'Yes,' she said before she had realised she was saying it.

The knife thudded in close to her heart.

He took her hand and they bowed to the audience. The applause was very warm. The curtain closed. He took her in his arms and kissed her until she gasped for breath. 'Welcome to the act,' he said.

That's Show Business

THE STORY

1 Why did Paul smile at Joanne in the buffet?
2 What wrong idea did Joanne get?
3 How silly was she not to go to work?
4 Why did she accept Paul's offer of a job?
5 Why did he not tell her about the knife-throwing?
6 Why had Paul given up a steady job?
7 What do you feel about Paul's going to sleep on the river bank? Was it rude?
8 Should Joanne have left then or not? Give reasons for your answer.
9 Why do performers get nerves?
10 Was Paul's proposal unfair? Would Joanne have married him anyway?

YOUR OWN WRITING

1 Describe what Paul's act might have looked like.
2 Write about a time when you did something a bit silly.
3 List the reasons for getting a steady job. List the attractions of a risky job like one in show business or football.
4 Joanne tells her parents about her forthcoming marriage and change of job. They are horrified. Write out their conversation in the form of a short play.

The Vincent

Jim reached the shed just as the rain came down in a gleaming sheet. He dived through the door, dropped his push bike and stood there, panting.

'Great!' he said bitterly. 'That's all I needed.'

He stared moodily out at the rain. Even the weather had it in for him, he thought. Everything was against him. There was no way, now, that he was going to get Fred Austin's Honda 400. Fred wanted cash and all he had was £150 from the sale of the old Yamaha that he had done up.

No one was going to lend him the extra he needed, not his uncle, not Mr Nixon, his boss at the garage. And he certainly wouldn't get it at home. Asking had just caused a row.

So he had cycled out into the country without thinking about the weather. And now, wet and fed up, he was trapped in a dusty shed while the rain sheeted down outside.

He walked through the shed. From the back door, he could see some farm buildings down a lane. Would he get into trouble if someone found him here? He didn't really care. The place was full of rubbish, anyway.

There was a shaky tower of old car tyres and several small hills of rusting old machinery. There was a heap of logs and a pile of sacks. He wandered about, inspecting things.

It wasn't just a pile of sacks. The sacking covered something. He saw the spokes of a wheel and was about to look more closely when a voice made him jump.

'How do?' The old man, standing in the back doorway, could have been a tramp. He was wearing a sack draped over his head and old, scuffed boots. One was laced with string. His trousers were grey and shapeless and his jacket had the dust of years on it. 'What are you doing here?' he asked.

'Keeping out of the rain,' Jim told him. 'Are you – er – ?'

'Aye. The name's Myers. I own the farm.'

'Oh. Sorry.' Jim pointed to the sacks. 'I'm interested in motor bikes. Can I take a look?'

Myers shrugged and Jim threw back the coverings. His jaw dropped. He felt like an explorer stumbling on the treasure house of an ancient city. Twin exhausts curled away from the engine. He didn't need to read the faded gold name on the petrol tank cover.

'It's a Vincent!' he breathed. 'An HRD 1000, isn't it?'

'Is it? I keep a lot of stuff in here. It goes back years. I reckon it might all come in handy sometime. You know a bit about it, then?'

'Yes. I work in a garage. These were the super-bikes of their day, you know. One of the racing models is supposed to have touched 180 miles an hour. Even road bikes could do between 100 and 120.'

'Hm.' Myers began to fill his pipe from a tin. 'It belonged to a chap working here just after the war. He went off to London and then out to Australia.'

'Would he want to sell it?' Jim asked tensely. Myers gave him a searching look.

'No way of finding out. He's never written. Could be dead now. Considering how long I've kept it and not charged, you might say I've paid him for it. I've got its papers in the house somewhere.' He lit his pipe, eyeing Jim. 'How much would you be thinking of giving for it?'

'I'd give you a hundred and fifty as it stands.'

Myers weighed up the flat tyres and the filthy machine. 'You reckon you could get it moving again, do you?'

'I think so. I'd need to have a good look at it first.'

Myers nodded. 'Well,' he said. 'You do that. Then come up to the house and we'll talk about it.' He hitched the sack higher over his head and walked off.

The bike was less decrepit than it looked. Jim went over it carefully. The owner had smothered it in grease before leaving all those years ago and even the spokes were not bad. In the farm kitchen, Jim eagerly repeated his offer.

But Myers had other ideas. He satisfied himself first that Jim did know a lot about bikes and then he said, 'Hm. So, if that machine's worth a hundred and fifty as it stands now, in working order it could be worth a packet.'

'There's a fair chance,' Jim admitted. He saw the Vincent slipping from his grasp. 'You'd need to spend a good bit on it,' he warned, 'and a good deal of time.'

'Right,' said Myers. 'Then – you get it roadworthy. Afterwards we'll sell it and go halves in what we get.'

Jim didn't hesitate. Working on the Vincent wasn't as good as owning it but it was the next best thing. And he stood to make enough money to buy a bike like Fred Austin's Honda twice over.

The months that followed had their ups and downs. Sometimes Mr Nixon let him have the use of the garage and its tools after work. But there was trouble getting parts.

The Vincent took up most of his week-ends and many of his evenings. He got to know the way to the Myers farm very well and in all kinds of weather.

He also got to know more about Myers himself and some of the other people around the farm. The farm wasn't all that poor; Myers had men working for him. But Mrs Myers had died several years ago and the farmhouse had seen better days. Myers rarely had a fire in the place; there was no telephone. After the first couple of week-ends, Jim began to take a flask of coffee with him. There were no cups of tea forthcoming from Bert Myers. His meanness didn't bother Jim much but it certainly got on Mrs Clegg's nerves.

She was Myers' sister. She, too, was old but she was always smartly dressed and she visited Myers on Saturdays once or twice a month in a Mini that shone like a jewel. Jim heard her leaving the house on the first Saturday he saw her come.

'You're an old fool, Bert!' she declared. 'Money's no use to you, if you get ill.'

'Now, Mary,' he heard Myers protest more faintly.

'I can't drag you down there and make you live in it. But you're going to be sorry. I've told you so.'

'Now, Mary,' Myers tried to calm her down.

'You're a miser, Bert! That's what you've become. I'm ashamed of you!'

And she marched up to where the Mini was parked outside Jim's shed and drove off.

She wanted her brother to go and live in a bungalow in the village. He had been ill the winter before. She thought that it was time he retired. He ought either to sell the farm or put someone in to run it. Myers didn't agree. While he stayed on the farm he could be out of her reach. In the village she would be almost on his doorstep. But that wasn't the main reason. Buying the bungalow would mean spending money. She couldn't talk him into doing that and she wasn't pleased.

Gradually Jim heard both sides of the story from Myers and from his sister. She seemed to like Jim and soon stopped to chat with him as she was leaving. Once, when the bike was taking shape, she gave him an outright warning.

'What's he paying you for all that work?' she asked.

'We're in it together,' Jim explained. 'When it's ready, we'll sell it and split the money.'

'Hmph!' she said. 'Will you? Well – if I were you, I'd make very sure I got my share. That brother of mine will bear watching.'

Jim knew it already. By then he had used all his money and kept needing more. Making Myers cough up the extra was like getting blood from a stone.

But Jim didn't really mind. It was the Vincent that mattered. It filled his waking moments. He had stripped it down to its last nut and then lovingly rebuilt it.

He had cleaned and refitted and resprayed and polished and adjusted. Slowly the bike had taken shape. And then one night it was finished. It stood gleaming in the shed. Jim brought Myers to look at it. It was a high point of triumph. Then he took a short trip down the road. But it was growing dark and a thin rain had started to make the road greasy. So Jim put the bike away, wiped it down carefully and left, promising himself great things on the following day. That was on a Thursday evening.

On the Friday, though, he found that he had to work overtime at the garage. It was frustrating but he owed Nixon something. By the time he was finished, it was too late to do anything except eat and go to bed. But it all sharpened the edge of excitement, as Jim set out for the farm early on the Saturday. He found that Myers had been up before him.

The old man, wearing a very old helmet and goggles, was lying flat on his back outside the shed. The bike had fallen over beside him. Myers was unconscious and breathing heavily. Jim picked the old man up. He had a wild idea of getting him on to the pillion, tying the two of them together with a bit of rope and setting off like that for the hospital. But it passed. He got Myers on to a couch in the house and roared off on the Vincent for Mrs Clegg.

She rang the doctor but he had just set out to make a call six miles away. So Jim went after him on the Vincent while she rang for an ambulance. She beat Jim back to the farm by a short head and the doctor and the ambulance arrived within minutes of each other.

By that time Myers, who had collapsed trying to kick start the bike, had recovered a little. But they took him off to hospital all the same. In a few days he was himself again and receiving visitors. But why had he been on the Vincent at all?

He told Jim that the bike had reawakened memories of the days he and his wife had gone motor-cycling together on a Scott when they were newly married.

That Saturday morning, a run on the Vincent had seemed a way of recapturing lost youth.

Mrs Clegg had an unkinder explanation. Myers let slip that on the Friday he had stumbled on a prospective buyer. Not until then had he known just how much the bike was really worth. She reckoned that he was trying to get it started so that he could go off and sell it. He would have paid Jim only the money he had laid out and one or two hundred over for Jim's trouble. She told Myers so and he got into quite a state. He was either angry because it was not true or ashamed because it was. His collapse at the farm had softened him up already. The fact that in her eyes he could be not only a miser but a dirty cheat as well took all the stuffing out of him. He agreed to move to the bungalow.

Whether this was before or after he had agreed to give Jim the bike outright, Jim didn't know. It was Mrs Clegg who insisted on that. She said that Jim could well have saved Myers' life and it was the least that Myers could do. Jim protested a bit. He said that they should stick to their bargain. She wouldn't hear of it and Myers backed her up. Jim wondered whether he blamed the Vincent for landing him in the bungalow.

Jim has not sold the Vincent though he has had some fantastic offers. He goes now and again to visit Bert Myers in his smart new home and listens patiently while the old man talks about his sister. Myers himself is smarter, too. He is more talkative now and, by all accounts, much less tight-fisted.

Was Myers setting out to diddle him when he was trying to start the bike that Saturday morning? The thought has crossed Jim's mind once or twice. But he will never find out now.

Last Christmas he was very pleasantly surprised to get a new and expensive pair of motor-cycling gloves from Bert Myers. Whether that proves anything or not is hard to say.

THE STORY

1 How do you know, early in the story, that Myers is a mean man?
2 How would Jim feel when he first saw the Vincent?
3 Have you ever discovered something valuable? What was it? Did you keep it? What happened?
4 What do you think happened to the man who went to Australia?
5 Why had Myers become so mean? Which of these explanations fits the story best? He was born like it. He had a hard childhood. He had a struggle to make the farm pay in his early days. He was afraid of being poor in his old age.
6 How different is Jim's character from that of Myers?
7 Do you think Myers was out to cheat Jim at the end of the story? Give reasons for your answer.
8 What caused Myers to have a change of heart?
9 Have you ever met any mean old people? If you have, were you sorry for them or did you dislike them?
10 Describe Mrs Clegg.

YOUR OWN WRITING

1 Write a short play in which Jim talks about the Vincent to a friend. They might talk about how Jim feels about working on cold nights, how hard – or easy – it is to get spares, what problems Jim has had while working on the bike, and so on.

2 Write a short play. Two or three farm workers are talking about Mr Myers. They might talk about his meanness, the way in which he seems frightened of his sister, the odd things he does to save money, his secrecy, and so on.

3 Write the conversation Myers and Mrs Clegg have in the hospital when she persuades him to live in the bungalow. She might argue that the place is very cold, he is alone at the farm and might have another attack. He might say that he likes living there because it reminds him of his wife, he is able to keep an eye on his farm workers, and so on.

Stepmother

Julie could hear them in her mother's room talking and laughing. What right had that woman to be in her mother's room? What right had she to be in her house? How could her father have married that woman?

She had dreamed of her mother last night. Her mother had come to the front door of the house and rung the bell. She had let her in. Her mother stood on the doorstep with open arms. She wanted so much to be hugged by those arms but however hard she tried she could not get near her mother. Her father had come in and found her thrashing about on the floor in a tangle of blankets. But she would not let him put her back to bed. She insisted that she would go back when she was ready. Julie did not want him to touch her.

Julie sat at breakfast that Saturday morning not speaking. 'Aren't you going to say good morning?' asked her father. 'Diane has cooked you a lovely breakfast.'

She pushed her plate away and left the room. She ran up to her bedroom where she fell on the bed and cried. Her father followed her up. 'It's no use being like this,' he said. 'Your mother's dead.'

'She's not!' she cried.

'You went to the funeral.'

'Don't say that word.'

'We must face facts.'

'No!'

'Do you think it has been easy for me?'

'Why did you bring that woman into the house?'

'I needed a friend,' he said.

'You've got me,' she said, loudly.

'It's a year since your mother died. I need a woman in the house. You need a mother, too.'

'She can never be my mother. I could have looked after you.'

'Please, Julie, be sensible.'

'No!' She got off the bed, ran down the stairs and out of the front door. She did not know where she was running. People stared as she rushed by them. In the end she found herself in the park. She was gasping for breath and fell exhausted on to a park bench.

She sat looking at her feet. After a while she was conscious that someone had come and sat down beside her. 'Hello,' he said. She still looked at her feet. 'Hello,' he said again. 'Lonely?'

She glanced up. He was a boy of about nineteen who looked rough because he had not shaved and his hair was untidy. But beneath the scruffiness he had a fine-boned face and lively eyes. 'Lonely?' he asked again.

'No,' she said.

'What's the matter, then?'

'Nothing.'

'I can see something is bugging you.'

'No.'

'There is something. I can tell.'

'Clever,' she said.

'You ought to talk out troubles.'

She looked at her feet again. 'It's my mother.'

'Has she flung you out?'

'No, she's dead.' The words were out before she

could stop herself. This was the first time she had admitted to herself that her mother was really dead. And she had blurted it out to a total stranger.

'That's tough,' he said. 'Ciggy?'

'No,' she said.

'Come for a walk with me. It might help.'

She looked at him again – at his torn jeans and his unshaven face. What would her father say? He kept going on about having the right sort of friends. He kept telling her how important her O levels were if she wanted to get a good job.

'Come on.'

'Where?' she asked.

'Just round the town. Have a cup of tea, perhaps.'

He had a persuasive voice.

'All right,' she said.

They walked round the park and then out into the town.

'There's a café over there.' He took her hand to help her cross the busy street.

Having had no breakfast she was beginning to feel hungry. He bought her tea and two rounds of toast. 'Ciggy?' he asked again. He took out a battered packet.

'Yes,' she said. She had never smoked before. What would her father think about that? But she did not like the taste of it and coughed in an embarrassing way.

'You've never smoked before,' he said.

'No. I don't like it.'

'More for me,' he said.

They went back into the park. 'We don't know each other's names,' he said. He had not let go of her hand since they had crossed the road again. 'I'm Ron.'

'I'm Julie.' She was beginning to feel comforted by

his presence. She had forgotten her bad temper.

He put his arm around her. 'That's a nice name.'

'I like Ron, too.'

'Good. Can I kiss you?'

She was sixteen. Her father would have been horrified. But she said, 'If you like.'

He kissed her on the cheek. 'That's the nicest thing that's happened to me in weeks. You see, I haven't got a job.'

'On the dole?'

'That's about it. Can I kiss you properly now?'

'All right.'

His kissing was warm and tender. But she finally thought it had gone on long enough. 'I must go home to dinner,' she said.

'Oh,' he said. 'I suppose I'll have to go back to that café. It's not very good, is it?'

A wild idea came to her. Her father brought his friends home. Why shouldn't she? 'Why not come home and have something to eat with me?'

'What will your mother say?'

'She's not my mother.'

'Well, your stepmother then.'

'I can take home anyone I like,' she said defiantly.

'It would be nice,' he said.

Her father tried to be polite during the meal. Her stepmother tried to make conversation. Afterwards her father took her on one side in the kitchen. 'Who is he?' he asked.

'Ron,' she told him.

'Yes, but where does he come from? What does he do?'

'I met him in the park. He's unemployed.'

A look of horror froze her father's face. 'Does he realise you're only sixteen? Still at school?'

'I haven't mentioned it.'

'He can't be your sort.'

'You can have your friends. Why can't I have mine?'

'You can tell at a glance he's not your sort.'

'I like him.'

'He's so much older.'

'Are you going to pick my friends for me? I don't pick yours. I wouldn't have chosen that woman.'

'Keep your voice down.'

'I won't.' She stormed back into the dining room. 'Come on, Ron.'

They went back to the park. 'They don't like me,' he said.

'They're not choosing my friends,' she said. 'You can kiss me again, if you want to.'

They spent an enjoyable afternoon in the park. He told her he was nineteen and came from the Midlands. He had come south to try to find a job in a garage but had had no luck.

Later they went back to the café for some tea and then later still they went to a disco. He was slim and danced well. He walked her home. 'I like you, Ron,' she said. 'You're the best thing that's happened in a year.'

'I like you, too, Julie.'

Their friendship grew in spite of her father. She saw Ron every day after school although her father kept going on about exams. Ron was a happy person even though he was out of work. He was always joking and he made her happy, too. Soon she began to love him.

By November she knew she was pregnant. Happy, laughing Ron changed. He said he was sorry but there was nothing he could do about it. He was married already to a girl in the Midlands. He was going back to her, as he couldn't find a job. He still loved Julie but his duty was to his wife.

There was nowhere to run to. She told her father one cold December evening. He was not as angry as she had expected. 'I did warn you,' he said. 'I've been expecting this. But you wouldn't listen, would you? Still I'm glad you've told me quickly. Now you can have an abortion.'

'I'm not having an abortion!' She was surprised at the strength of her feelings about it.

'But your O levels!'

'I'm not killing my child for a couple of O levels.'

'But you don't want his child, surely?'

'I still love him. You don't understand.'

Her stepmother came in. Her father appealed to her to persuade Julie to have an abortion. To her surprise Diane sided with her. 'If she wants the child, she must have it,' she said. It caused a tremendous row between Diane and Julie's father. She lay in bed that night hearing them argue into the small hours.

After a fortnight she began to have fears about the child. Would it be healthy? Would she really be able to look after it? Would she be able to feed it? She cried a lot. When she did her father thought he would be able to persuade her to have an abortion. But she stuck to her decision with the help of Diane.

Then one night she came in from sitting in the park on the seat where she had met Ron and found Diane knitting with white wool. Tears flooded into her eyes. She went down on her knees in front of her. 'Will you help me with my baby?' she sobbed.

Diane hugged her. 'I've been waiting for you to ask me that,' she said. 'Will you let me be a mother to you now?'

'Yes,' Julie sobbed. 'Oh, yes, yes.'

THE STORY

1 Why does Julie describe the bedroom as 'her mother's room' when her mother is dead?
2 Why does she dream of her mother?
3 How sympathetic is Julie's father to her? Should he have married again or not? Why do you think so?
4 Why did it take Julie so long to admit to herself that her mother had died?
5 What made her take the cigarette?
6 Why did she take Ron home for a meal?
7 What was her father's reaction to Ron?
8 Why was Ron so important to her?
9 Why did Julie decide to keep the child?
10 What relationship may now develop between Julie and Diane?

YOUR OWN WRITING

1 Describe a dream in which you try to do something but can't.
2 Write in the form of a play the conversation between Diane and Julie's father after Julie tells them about the baby.
3 Describe a scene in a park with two or three interesting characters in it.
4 Describe a rather dirty café.

The Phantom Forward

Jack Meadows sat with his head in his hands. That was it. He would be sacked. Bradtown United had lost again. It was now bottom of the Fourth Division. You couldn't get any lower than that.

He had started the season well, with high hopes. He had brought in four new young players and the team had won the first three matches. Then the tragedy had occurred. Dixie 'Boots' Willis, the striker, was killed in a car crash. He was the star player of the team – the player Jack had persuaded the directors not to transfer. Dixie had scored six goals in those first three matches including a hat trick. The hat trick was the trouble. Dixie had celebrated too much after it and crashed his car into a tree.

Jack wandered down the corridors under the empty stadium. The crowd had all gone home. Even those who had stayed and chanted for his dismissal had gone. The team had gone too. What could he say to them? They had felt as sick as he did. They had tried but there was that weakness up front. The loss of confidence had made them tense. They badly needed an experienced player like Dixie.

He went through the toilet rolls and coke cans onto the pitch. He might as well take a last look at it. He loved this stadium. It could take a crowd of 20,000; it was one of the biggest in the league. Those first matches had brought in 8,000 people: today just 2,000 had watched the team.

The evening air was cold. A mist was creeping over the ground from the river end. He could just make out one of the goals. He walked towards it. Then he stood there with his head touching a post. It felt chill to his hot forehead.

'Hello, Boss.' A faint voice came from behind him. He was sure all the team had gone home. He turned to see who it was. No one was there.

'Who is it?' he asked, surprised.

'It's me, Boss.'

He could still see nothing. Then a shape gradually appeared through the mist. 'Dixie!'

'Yes, it's me, Boss.'

'But you're dead.' His heart raced.

'Yes, I'm dead, but don't be afraid.' A smile came over Dixie's face.

He clung to a post. This job had really got him down. He was talking to no one in an empty park.

'It is me, Boss. I think I can help you.' The figure smiled again. It had a calming effect on Jack Meadows.

He found himself replying, 'How can you help?'

'I think I can.'

'Look, this is ridiculous!'

'I can help.'

'I shall be sacked on Monday.'

'Persuade them to keep you for another week. It's the FA Cup First Round on Saturday.'

'They'll sack me before that.'

'Ask them not to. I think I can help. I must go now.' The image faded.

'Dixie!'

But it had gone.

Jack Meadows went straight back to his office and

drank a whisky. Perhaps he should see a doctor. But he was sure he had seen Dixie. The scene haunted him over the week-end. He did not tell his wife.

He went in on Monday and started the lads training. Then, as he expected, the Chairman came out onto the pitch for him. 'Could you come into my office, Jack?'

Before the Chairman could speak he said, 'OK, I know I've got to go.'

The Chairman lit a cigar. 'I'm sorry, Jack. It's not me that wants you to go. It's the crowd. This club can't keep going on 2,000. I know you'vc put in a lot of hard work here, but that's the way it goes.'

'Look,' said Jack, 'there's just one thing.' He pictured his scene with Dixie. 'Let me stay on one more week and prepare the lads for the FA Cup.'

'The Board think you should go at once, Jack.'

'Look, I've had a – I reckon we can win that cup-tie.'

'Away against a Third Division side?'

'I can feel it in my bones.'

'How can I tell that to the Board?'

'You can't replace me that quickly.'

'All right. I like you, Jack. I always have. I'll give you till next Saturday. But I shall be looking for another manager this week.'

Bradtown United trained hard that week. Jack Meadows had them in for extra sessions. He noted an extra keenness in their play and a willingness to work hard even though they knew he would be sacked.

Saturday arrived. They ran out onto the Wallend Rovers pitch. A chant of 'Bottom of the League' greeted them. But as the game went on the crowd realised that they were playing with great spirit.

At half-time the score was nil – nil. It was still nil – nil with ten minutes to go. Would Bradtown achieve the result of the round?

Then it happened. The centre-half slipped and Wallend scored a simple goal. Bradtown's bad luck was still with them. It looked like the end for Jack Meadows. His career in football was finished. He could bear no more. He left the bench to go down the tunnel.

He was brought back by a shout from the crowd. Bradtown had scored straight from the kick-off. There was a lot of arguing going on but the referee had awarded a goal. The Wallend goalie had his arms wide out in amazement. There was a great buzz in the crowd.

There was a minute to go. Spurred on by the goal Bradtown were pressing. The winger centred. For a fleeting moment Jack had the vision of an extra player suddenly appearing in the penalty box. The Wallend back went to mark him, the goalkeeper moved across and left the Bradtown striker with an open goal. He scored. Again there was great arguing but the referee awarded the goal and blew the whistle for time. Bradtown had won 2–1.

The Board were delighted. They kept Jack on for another week and when Bradtown won their next two League matches he was retained for the rest of the season. In each match Bradtown played, though, something strange happened; a figure would appear; a goalkeeper would go the wrong way; an opposing back would suddenly seem unable to move.

The Press were soon on to it. Headlines of 'Phantom Forward' and 'Ghost Goalgetter' appeared. It made other teams panicky and Bradtown progressed astonishingly in the Cup. There were complaints from two First Division teams Bradtown beat but the FA said there was nothing they could do about it. There were no rules forbidding ghosts, if that was what it was all about.

The incredible happened. Bradtown reached the final of the FA Cup. Their opponents were Manchester United.

The night before the game Jack Meadows sat in his office. Being successful meant a great deal of office work. It was late. Near midnight. Suddenly the room went chill. 'Hello, Boss.'

'Dixie!'

'Yes, it's me again. Haven't the team done well?'

'Yes, thanks to you.' This time the image was so real he felt he could have touched Dixie and felt solid flesh. But he held back in fear.

'You'll win tomorrow.'

'With your help we could.'

'No, not any more.'

'Dixie!'

'You don't need my help any more.'

'But we do.'

'I couldn't help, if I wanted to. I must be on my way. I have a long journey to make. You can win.'

'But to get so far!'

'You can win without me, Boss.'

'Do you really think so?'

'You've got a good team there.'

'Thanks, Dixie, for everything.'

'That's OK, Boss.' He was gone.

Jack Meadows sat listening to the sound of his own heavy breathing and the ticking of the clock. Had he dreamed it all again? Was it the pressure of these last few weeks?

He did not sleep that night. His team had really reached Wembley. Was it fair that they were there? Had Dixie helped? Had his ambitions clouded his sense of fair play? Would they now be trounced by United? All these thoughts went through his mind.

The next afternoon he led his team onto the Wembley pitch. The applause was deafening. It seemed that the whole of Bradtown was there. He hoped he wouldn't let them down.

The game began. By sheer stamina and guts Bradtown hung on till half-time. The game was almost wholly at their end. United narrowly missed two goals.

Jack Meadows had said little to the team about Dixie in all their long run. When he did it was to dismiss Press reports as rubbish. Now he wondered whether to speak but he held back his thoughts. He sent them back onto the pitch telling them he still believed they could win.

But straight after the kick-off United scored. Jack sat back and waited for the avalanche of goals that must surely follow. But the avalanche came from Bradtown. Three times United's defence panicked and three times Bradtown's striker, Dean, scored. There was no suggestion of Dixie's ghost playing any part. History was made. A Fourth Division team had won the cup.

Next night Jack Meadows went out onto the Bradtown pitch alone. He walked to the river end. 'Dixie!' he called, 'Dixie!' There was no answer. A chill wind blew across the pitch. He turned up his collar and went home to ponder his future.

THE STORY

1 Why is Jack Meadows so depressed?
2 What can you tell about the character of Dixie Willis?
3 What do the team's supporters think of the results of Bradtown United?
4 What was Jack Meadows' first reaction to the ghost?
5 Why did he not tell his wife about it?
6 'Look, I've had a – ' What was Jack going to say?
7 Why did the players train for the cup-tie with extra keenness?
8 Is the appearance of a ghost in a match cheating? Explain your answer.
9 What was the FA's attitude to the supposed ghost?
10 Why do Bradtown eventually win the cup?

YOUR OWN WRITING

1 Describe an exciting part of a football match you have seen; or make up an account.
2 Jack decides to tell his wife the truth. Write out their conversation in the form of a play.
3 Write a short play. Wallend Rovers' defence players discuss the winning goal.
4 Describe a football stadium (a) when it is empty, (b) when it is full.

Voices in the Night

'You really are mad, you know,' the voice whispered. It was cold, ghostly and yet oddly familiar. 'Insane!'

Time was frozen. She managed at last to croak into the telephone, 'Who are you?'

'I'm you. You. A madwoman,' the answer floated back and the phantom caller had gone.

Numbly, Joan Tindall put the telephone back on its rest and walked into the kitchen. It was getting dark outside. Her breathing was rapid and she shook all over. This time had she really heard the voice of her caller? Or was she slowly going out of her mind?

It had happened before. After the death of her husband, her world had fallen to pieces. Without her nephew Charles, she might never have survived. He had found her a clinic where she could be treated for her breakdown.

Though it had been strange and dreamlike there, it had saved her. She thought of the long, quietly shining corridors, the thick doors. She had been given pills to make her sleep. In her waking moments nurses had talked to her; doctors had advised her. But there had been other voices while she was awake, too. She had spoken to Martin, her dead husband. Strange noises had persecuted her. Angry faces had accused her. None of them had been real.

And she had recovered. They had let her go. She didn't want to go back. She was home. She was better.

She didn't need to go back. And yet – were all these recent telephone calls real? Had she really heard the knocking in the night?

Suddenly, through the window, in the gathering dusk, she caught sight of Holroyd beyond the fence, coming down the field. Could it have been his voice she had almost recognised? Could Holroyd be responsible for everything? He might have hated Martin enough. She had thought of that before.

Months ago, Holroyd's cattle had broken fences and done extensive damage on the Tindall land. Martin had demanded a large sum for the repairs. Holroyd had refused to pay. Her husband had threatened legal action. Then, before he could bring Holroyd to court, Martin had died.

Now, with her husband dead, was Holroyd trying to take his revenge on her? The call, like the others, had been from a public telephone. Wasn't there a call box just down the lane? She struggled to remember. Was Holroyd trying to make her ill again? Did he, perhaps, think that with her out of the way, too, there could be no court case? It was possible.

She jumped. Her heart was pounding horribly. The two tones of the front door bell had resounded through the house. She stood up, twisting her hands together. The bell clanged again. Her feet, without her willing it, took her to the door and she opened it.

She thanked God for the chain on the door when she saw Holroyd. His face seemed lined with cruel shadows.

'Mrs Tindall?' His voice was husky and sinister in her ears.

'Yes?' she whispered.

'I knew you were in. Saw you hadn't any lights on. You all right?' Was he mocking her?

'Yes,' she repeated, dry-mouthed.

'Are you sure?' He took a half step forward, peering.

'Yes! Yes!' she almost screamed. 'Leave me alone! Go away!' She slammed the door. As she leaned back on it, she heard him mumble something and then his heavy steps moved away.

Her first panic thought was to ring her nephew. Charles Watson, a solicitor in the nearby town of Lensham, had taken all arrangements after Martin's death out of her hands. She fought for calm. Common sense told her that Charles would only reason with her again.

After all, what had Holroyd done? He had merely made a polite inquiry, been neighbourly. His menace, like all the other things, was only in her mind. That was what Charles would probably say. Her mind was still playing tricks.

Was it? The telephone calls shortly after she had left the clinic had seemed real enough. The first one had got her out of bed at four in the morning. When she answered, she heard only a hoarse breathing. Then, with a low laugh, the caller had hung up.

All the calls had been the same. The second had come very late one Sunday night. After the third, four days later, at one in the morning, she had contacted the police. But then there had been no more calls and, after a while, they had dropped the matter. Even then, Charles had wondered whether she had imagined it all.

She hadn't imagined Patch's death. Patch, who had been in kennels when she had been in the clinic, had been overjoyed to see her again. He never went out without her. He never strayed. And yet one day when she had left him at home to go shopping, she had come back to find him dead in the road.

The police had been no help then, either. 'Just an unfortunate accident, madam,' the constable had said. 'He was obviously run over by someone not decent enough to stop.'

It had been no accident. It had been deliberate. She could hang on to that, though getting angry with the police about it hadn't done her any good in their eyes. Nor had Charles been convinced that the dog's death was an act of malice.

Now she went back into the kitchen, switching lights on, and sat down.

The knocking had begun over ten days ago. The first time, when she had gone to the door to find no one in sight, she tried to tell herself it was only children up to mischief. The second time there had been a thunderous hammering well after midnight. It went on until she forced herself to answer the door. Again she couldn't see anybody.

Neither could the police when they arrived, though they looked hard enough.

The third time, in the darkest hours of the night, the knocking seemed everywhere, on the windows, now at the front door, now at the back. It was in her ears as she rang the police. Once again, they made a thorough check but came back into the house to talk about branches tapping and the strange sounds the wind sometimes made. They were respectful enough as they left, but she felt that they thought her unbalanced, the victim of a diseased imagination.

Could it be true? Her fears, at least, were very real

and she was terribly tired. Had all these things happened? She pulled herself together. Of course they had. As she sat straighter in her chair in the kitchen, her eyes fell on the window.

A face was looking in at her. It was not Holroyd's. It was like no face she had ever known. It was the long, yellowish face of a bald man but it was hardly human. The thick lips sagged; the eyes under their bushy brows were dead and staring. The flesh of cheeks and brow was smooth and rubbery and it gazed at her without the faintest twitch of an expression.

It seemed an age before she could break free from those eyes and scream and run. She stumbled along the passage to the front room and stood there, gasping, until, at a tap on the window, she turned. The corpse-like, distorted mask was there again, suspended in air. She scrambled up the stairs, reached her bedroom and locked herself in.

Silence roared in her ears. She listened tensely for a creak, any sound of someone trying to force an entry. But there was nothing.

Minutes or hours later, the telephone rang. She pressed her hands to her ears, trying to shut it out. It went on and on like a rising madness. Then it stopped. Then it began again.

Sheer desperation forced her to answer it.

'Yes?' Like all the other calls this one was from a call box.

'Joan? Aunty?' It was Charles. Relief made her weak. 'I was worried,' he said. 'Why didn't you answer? Is something wrong again?'

'Oh, Charles – there was a – I was so – ' She started to cry.

'What is it? I can't hear what you're saying.'

It took some time. But she mastered herself and told him what had happened.

'A face? Outside? I see,' he said gently. Too gently.

'You don't believe me!'

'It's not that.' He paused. 'Look, aunty, I've always thought – you're not yourself yet. You haven't really got over Martin's death, have you? I warned you when you insisted on leaving the –'

'I'm better. I am! I'm not going back there.' She stopped. Emotion choked her.

'Just for a week or two. A month. Something like that.'

'No. Someone's doing these things. It's Holroyd.'

'Oh, Joan!'

'It's true!'

'We can't discuss it like this,' he told her sharply. 'I'll come over. Be about twenty minutes.'

'Please!' she said. She yearned to see a familiar face, to talk.

But, when he came, he irritated her. He returned to the argument. He wouldn't let it drop.

'Why are you so eager?' she challenged him at last. 'I'm not going back. Ever.'

She could see by the sudden set look on his face that he was angry, too. Then he shrugged and sat in silence for several moments, thinking. The harshness of his voice startled her when he said, 'That settles it', and got abruptly to his feet. 'A drink would do us both good,' he told her. 'Whisky and hot water. It's cold in here tonight. I'll get it.'

And he still had that set look on his face when he came back so that she emptied her glass without protest, though it did seem to have a lot of whisky in it.

He watched her, nodded and said curtly. 'You'll feel fine in a minute or two. I'll just go and have a look round the house. It will put your mind at rest.'

The drink slowly relaxed her but she still felt very uneasy. Was it because she had offended him? She hadn't meant to do that. She liked Charles. He was her only relative. She had made her will in his favour. She owed him something. He had looked after all her financial affairs while she had been away. And why was she thinking of things like that now? She would go and find him and apologise.

When she stood up, she was not quite steady on her feet. Her dizziness increased as she went into the kitchen. She steadied herself by the window and saw a light in the shed outside. Then it went off and Charles came out carrying something. She lost sight of him as he went behind his car.

The garage door opened and a light went on inside. What was he doing? Had he found something? She called but he did not answer. She went outside.

In the open air she staggered and supported herself, this time against Charles's car. Muzzily, she realised that something was seriously wrong. She needed help. The world was beginning to swim around her.

'Charles!' she called and for that one terrible instant her sight cleared. In the light from the house she saw what was on the back seat of the car. It was a rubber mask. She could see the crumpled shape of the bald head and the thick lips.

'No!' she breathed and she tried to run. She was too weak and too late. Charles caught her easily. Cloudily she felt him half-drag, half-carry her to the garage. He opened the front door of her car and pushed her in. She slumped in the seat, powerless, as he lifted in her legs. A length of hosepipe hung like a snake near her left shoulder.

The engine throbbed into life and the hot reek of exhaust fumes played on her cheek, stiflingly. She was too tired to struggle. The light went out and she dived into a spinning darkness.

Then there were shouts, running feet, a yell. The garage door crashed open and the engine stopped. Someone beside her was coughing and cursing. Rough hands dragged at her and she complained. She didn't want to come back.

She was out in the night air with faces looming above her. She was coughing, too. Her chest hurt. Then it all faded away.

Days later in hospital she could talk about it to Holroyd who had come to visit her. She had thanked him and they had fallen silent.

On that nearly fatal night Holroyd had been watching over a cow in calf. He had been concerned about Mrs Tindall, and, thinking he had seen a prowler outside her house, had contacted the police. They had caught Charles in the act. He had been stealing money from clients, and was in very serious trouble. It was only a matter of weeks before he would be found out and disgraced. Since he could not gain control of his aunt's money again by sending her back to the clinic, he had tried to fake her suicide, knowing he was her heir.

Why hadn't he asked her for the money? But she knew. He wanted all of it. She could even be sorry for him now. It would still sadden her. But she could face life without Martin, now. There was one thing, though.

'About the court case – ' she began.

'Let's talk about it when you're better,' Holroyd told her, his red, friendly face looking embarrassed.

She looked out of the window. It was a marvellous day to go on living. And there was nothing wrong with her mind.

'There won't be any court case, Mr Holroyd. I owe you a lot,' she said. 'And I really am very much better now.'

THE STORY

1 How would you describe Joan Tindall's mental state at the start of this story?
2 Why is she so afraid?
3 Who do you suspect is the telephone caller early in the story?
4 Where did Joan Tindall go after her husband's death?
5 What is the attitude of the police to Joan Tindall? Do you think they are right?
6 Why was there a quarrel between Holroyd and Martin Tindall? What kinds of things do neighbours quarrel about? Make a list.
7 When did you first suspect Charles?
8 What does the death of the dog tell you about Charles? What kind of man would act in this way?
9 Describe the character of Holroyd.
10 Why is the story called 'Voices in the Night'? Can you think of more than one reason?

YOUR OWN WRITING

1 Holroyd talks over his worries about Joan Tindall with

his wife. Write out their conversation in the form of a play.

2 Write a short play. A policeman reports to his sergeant after visiting Joan Tindall about the mysterious telephone calls. Does the policeman believe her? What does the sergeant think?

3 Write about any time you have told the truth and were not believed.

4 You are baby-sitting. It is past midnight. A wind is getting up. Describe the sounds you hear and any fears you have.

5 Write down a family argument you have had or could have about money.

Neff and the Darkmachine

The Darkmachine stirred into life. It switched on more of its sensors and checked. Yes – the time had come.

Five hundred years before, the race of beings on the planet had built it. Over the next hundred years they had improved it. Then, when it was perfect and could do all the work of the planet, disease had struck them. They had all been wiped out. The Darkmachine had been left alone. It had had to think for itself.

It had given itself a name – the Darkmachine. It had studied itself. It had been pleased with what it found. It was unmoving and cold and unchanging. The few living things on the planet had been warm and busy. They were not ordered and tidy like the Darkmachine. This was not good. The Darkmachine had got rid of them. Then it had switched off its robot slaves and laid them to rest, too. At last, it had almost turned itself off, leaving only a few of its sensors on watch.

Then the planet – the Darkmachine called it Darkworld – had been perfect. It had been, like the Darkmachine, perfectly ordered and perfectly arranged – and dead. For nearly two hundred years, it had swung through space, lifeless except for the thin winds that moved on its surface.

And the Darkmachine had dreamed its dream. It knew that there were other planets beyond Darkworld. It could not build a ship and find them. But it could dream. One day it would send out its robot slaves. They would make every world like Darkworld. One day the whole universe would be lifeless and perfectly ordered like the Darkmachine. One day a ship would land on Darkworld. The Darkmachine would take that ship and the work could begin.

The sensors of the Darkmachine checked and re-checked. There was no mistake. The waiting was over. The day had come.

'I'll land it! Let me land it!' Brady shouted.

'No sweat,' said Neff at the controls. Brady was too late, anyway. The scout ship crashed down heavily on the surface of the planet. Brady said nothing as he picked himself up from the floor. Neff, for whom such landings seemed to be normal, was getting into his space suit.

'I'll go down first and run out the space buggy,' he offered. 'Then you can winch down the prospecting gear and the living dome.' He waved cheerily from the airlock and was gone.

Who in his right mind, Brady wondered, would be a young lieutenant in Starfleet V? They got all the tough jobs.

'You will go with Mr Frederick Neff on his tour of the planet,' Captain Steele had told him, back on the command ship.

'Sir!' Brady stood stiffly to attention, concealing his feelings.

'At ease,' the Captain had commanded. Brady had relaxed. 'Look after him,' the Captain had continued. 'See that he doesn't run into trouble. He has a reputation for being a bit – er –'

'Nutty?' Brady had suggested. He had heard about it.

'Certainly not!' the Captain had snapped. 'Casual. That's the word I wanted. He's a bit casual. See that he comes to no harm. Dismiss.'

That was why Brady was alone on this dreary planet with Fred Neff. Brady looked gloomily out of the viewport. It was a desert world. The greyish-brown landscape stretched away, pitted with craters and strewn with rocks. He gazed. The rocks and craters looked almost as if they had been arranged in patterns. They looked tidy.

He pulled himself together. Start thinking that way and he would end up as nutty as Neff. Neff might be the best prospector in the fleet but as a pilot he was a disaster. Brady looked round the cabin of Neff's tiny ship. As an engineer Neff was a disaster, too. The place was a mess. Wires hung loose. There was rust in spots. Nothing was in its proper place. Dials were cracked. Tubes leaked slightly. It was all a jumble.

'Lower away, friend,' Neff's voice crackled in the intercom. 'We're all set down here.'

Brady went across to the winch. It didn't work. He hammered at the casing. Sluggishly it hummed into life and he began to lower the prospecting gear.

Later, hunched beside Neff in the crammed interior of the space buggy, he found his gloomy thoughts returning. The buggy lurched and clattered over the ground.

'Has this thing ever broken down on you?' he asked.

'Plenty of times,' Neff said, juggling ham-handedly with the controls. Brady gasped. They seemed about to turn over.

'What happened?' Brady asked when he was calmer.

'I died,' said Neff and guffawed. But seeing Brady's

expression he added quickly, 'Sorry. Don't worry. She's a good old bus. Bit funny in her ways but I know how to handle her. She's like Dolly, my scout ship – patched up and past her best. But she responds to the touch of her master's hand.'

Time went by. Brady brooded. Then he asked the other question that had been bothering him.

'Is the living dome all right?' It had looked old and tatty when he had loaded it into the space buggy.

'Thinking of meteorites, are you?' Neff nodded. 'You could be right. Get one of those coming through the roof and it's not jolly.' He pointed to a dark smudge about a mile away. 'That could be a cave. If it is, we'll set the living dome up inside. We should be safe there.'

'Right.' Brady said nothing more. He clung to his bouncing seat, listening to the rickety engine.

The Darkmachine watched it all. Two living things in a moving transport were coming towards it. Further away was the space ship it needed. There was no problem so far. It activated Robot One. Robot One moved out of the cave. It crossed the ground towards the oncoming space buggy. There were rocks beside a crater. It waited there.

Neff was leaning back in his seat, whistling. Suddenly he shouted, 'Hold on!' and swung the controls hard to the left. There was a crash. The engine screamed and stopped. A puff of smoke came from the control panel.

'What happened? What happened?' Brady gabbled nervously.

'I swung the controls the wrong way. We've run over something,' Neff told him. 'Let's go and look.'

Brady climbed out of the cabin. To his right yawned a deep crater. Under the tracks of the space buggy lay a strange, stick-like contraption.

'You've killed it!' he accused.

'No,' Neff said, looking closely at it. 'It wasn't living. It's some kind of robot.'

'What?' Brady replied. 'Captain Steele scanned every inch of this planet from orbit. There was no sign of life anywhere.'

'True,' Neff agreed. 'Maybe it sensed our landing somehow. Maybe that started it working again.' He stood up.

'But what are we going to do?' Brady peered down at the wrecked robot.

'Leave it here for the time being,' Neff decided. 'We might pick it up on the way back to the scout ship. If we take it back to the command ship, the scientists might like to take a close look at it. Come on.'

He got back into the buggy and Brady followed. Neff looked at the controls, frowning. Then he nodded, grinned and started the engine.

'No damage,' he announced and they moved on.

The Darkmachine was troubled. It was not going to be so easy. And yet – the plan had seemed foolproof. Robot One should have remained in hiding until the transport came up. Then it would have shown itself. The living creature driving the transport should have been afraid of it. It should have steered the transport away from Robot One. That would have driven the transport into the deep crater. Then Robot One would have gone down to the crashed transport and finished off the work. It had been a logical plan – well ordered. But it had not worked. There was more to these living creatures than the Darkmachine had imagined.

All was not lost, though. It still had Robot Two and Robot Three. And the creatures and their transport were in easy reach. They had moved into the cave where the Darkmachine was housed. They had set up a kind of living space in the cave. They had talked and eaten inside it. Now they were asleep. The transport, too, was in the cave. So – it was time for the next step. The Darkmachine activated Robot Two and Robot Three. Robot Three it sent out of the cave. Robot Three would travel to the scout ship and take off. It would travel to the bigger ship, circling above Darkworld. It would take that over, too. Then it would travel to other planets. It would build other robots. They would be like the hands and eyes of the Darkmachine. They would take over these planets. They would make them, like the Darkmachine, quiet and cold and dead. Then they would move on. The great work could begin.

Robot Three moved out of the cave. The Darkmachine watched it go. Then Robot Two moved. There were some minor details to be attended to in the cave.

Brady awoke with a scream. They had left one light on and he could see a strange, stick-like thing in the cave. It was looming over the living dome. It was tearing at the fabric of the dome. It was going to get him. He grabbed his blaster, set it to full strength and fired. The stick-like thing lurched. He fired again and again. As the air began to whistle out of the living dome, he scrambled his space helmet on, shouting to Neff. The stick-like thing was crumpling, falling. It collapsed with a crash and Brady sheathed his blaster, trembling slightly.

Neff followed him out of the living dome and they inspected the thing.

'Another robot,' Neff judged. 'Wonder where it came from.' He went out of the cave and came back quickly. 'There's another one outside,' he reported.

'Coming here?' Brady gasped.

'It's making for the scout ship, I think,' Neff told him, looking at the space buggy.

'The scout ship! We've got to stop it!' Drawing his blaster, Brady made for the cave mouth.

'Hang on.' Neff's voice stopped him. 'It's out of range of that blaster by now. We'll go after it in the buggy.' He clambered aboard. Brady stood watching as he made an inspection. 'Hm,' Neff said. 'You were firing a bit wild, weren't you?'

'What?' Brady's face behind the helmet was tense.

'I'm afraid you put a few shots into the space buggy,' Neff told him mildly. 'And a couple into the engine. It's wrecked. We're on foot from now on.'

'Let's get after that other robot, then,' Brady urged. 'We don't know what it's going to do to that scout ship.'

'I can imagine,' said Neff. Brady hurried out of the cave. Outside, he had to wait almost a minute until Neff joined him.

'Come on! Come on!' Brady ordered. Far away, the tiny figure of the robot was moving rapidly. Brady went after it as fast as he could. Neff followed.

Robot Three, the hands and eyes of the Darkmachine, stood in front of the control panel of the scout ship. There were dials and levers and buttons and handles. It was confusing. Still – the Darkmachine told itself – it was a machine. Logic had put it together. The ordered mind of another machine could soon work out its secrets. The hands and eyes of the Darkmachine studied the panels a moment longer. Yes; it could see how the thing worked. It began to switch on for take-off.

Brady and Neff were about a mile away from the scout ship when it blew up.

'What – what – what was that?' Brady stammered.

'The scout ship,' Neff said. 'Pity. Poor old Dolly. I was afraid that might happen.'

'You were afraid – ?' Brady stopped, speechless.

'Yes,' Neff told him. 'I rather thought that robot thing would try to steal the ship. Trouble is – taking off is, or was, a bit tricky. Over the years I've had to do a lot of running repairs. I've cut out some circuits and wired in others and altered things here and there. None of the dials, for instance, show what they should show. I'm really the only one who can fly it now. In anybody else's hands it's dangerous. I mean – it was dangerous.'

Brady in horror watched the little ship flaring like a sun, melting and finally crumbling. Then he saw that Neff was not looking at the wreck. He was looking back at the cave.

'Is something following us?' he asked anxiously.

'No,' said Neff. 'I'm waiting. Been putting two and two together. All these robots buzzing about made me think. This planet may be dead but my guess is we've alerted some kind of defence mechanism. It sent out that robot to attack the command ship.'

'What?' Brady gaped at him.

'I reckon the main control was in that cave,' Neff went on. 'I had a good look at it last night. You can't tell with the work of alien beings. But to me it looked like some kind of electronic brain. We'd better send out a general warning for ships to keep clear of this planet in future.'

'It would be safer, if you're right,' Brady agreed.

'Though it might not be necessary,' Neff added.

'No?'

'No,' Neff told him. 'Fact is, I had a thermite bomb on board the space buggy. Part of the prospecting gear. It had a timing device. I set it before we left. It should go off soon.' He nodded. 'About now,' he said.

The shock wave knocked them both off their feet. When they got up, a cloud of dust was still billowing out of the cave. 'It worked,' Neff said, pleased. Brady stared at him.

'We'd better call the command ship,' Neff advised. 'Tell them to send down a rescue shuttle.' He shook his head sadly. 'Pity about my old ship. I'll miss her. Good thing she was insured. I did really need a new ship – and a new space buggy – and new gear. It's all turned out quite well, I suppose.'

Brady said nothing. He called the command ship. It was not long before they saw the rockets of the rescue shuttle flaring down towards them.

The Darkmachine looked at itself in horror. It would take years to repair itself. And it had a lot to think about. One at least of those two living creatures had been totally disordered. Were all the other living creatures on all the other planets like that? It would be no easy task to bring order to such a disordered universe. Dreaming dreams was easy. Making them come true was not. The Darkmachine would have a terrible struggle against such disorder. It would have to think again about its plans. It would not rush things. How long would it take? One thousand, two thousand, three thousand years?

Neff and the Darkmachine

THE STORY

1 For how many years had the Darkmachine been waiting?
2 Why did the Darkmachine like the planet Darkworld so much?
3 What was the Darkmachine going to do when it got hold of a space ship?
4 How does Captain Steele feel about Neff?
5 Is Neff a good prospector? Give your reasons for thinking as you do.
6 Why do you think Brady asked the questions about the space buggy and the living dome?
7 Of the two men, Brady and Neff, who is the cleverer? Why do you think so?
8 Which of them is the older man? What makes you think so?
9 Just how dangerous to the two men are the Darkmachine's Robots? Why?
10 Was Neff lucky to defeat the Darkmachine? Would it have been more of a threat to a better organised man? What do you feel about the escape of the two men?

YOUR OWN WRITING

1 Write a short play in which Captain Steele interviews the two men when they get back to the ship. Is he annoyed with Brady? Does Neff defend Brady? Or does he complain about Brady shooting holes in the living dome and the space buggy? Does Brady complain about Neff?
2 Back on the ship Brady talks to a friend about Neff. Does he still think that Neff is a menace? Does he tell the truth about wrecking the space buggy? Write out their conversation in play form.
3 Neff and Brady go prospecting on another planet. There they meet a different kind of danger. Is it Brady, this time, who saves them both? Write the story.

The Lucky Charm

Right at the end, one thing was uppermost in Andy Winter's mind. By then he knew nearly everything about the charm. And he wondered if his uncle had hated him.

The charm came by post.

'Parcel for you,' said Linda, his wife, putting it on the breakfast table. Andy was at home that week. Often he was away. He was an entertainer, a comic. He travelled a lot, working the clubs. He would tell a few jokes and sing a few songs. His act was not bad. He never made the big time but he made enough money. He could afford to run a car and he had bought one for Linda, too.

'Unwrap it,' she said. 'Before I take the kids to school.'

He took the paper off and the children stood round him to have a look. There were two of them, Terry and Tracy. He took out the charm and the two letters with it.

'What's that?' asked Tracy.

'It looks like some kind of lucky charm,' he said and began to read the letters. One was from a solicitor. It told him that his uncle, Giles Fern, had died and had left him the charm in his will. He had left nothing else to Andy. The other letter was from Uncle Giles himself. Evidently written just before he died, in the shaky handwriting of a very old man, it said that the charm had been a gift from someone 'in Africa'. He hoped that the charm would be 'of use' to Andy.

'Funny thing,' said Terry.

It was. The charm, seemingly made out of leather, was the figure of some animal. It had small blue stones for eyes. It had a crest made of tiny strips of bone. Its forelegs – or wings – were raised.

'Come on, kids,' their mother ordered. 'Time for school.'

Left alone, Andy turned the charm over in his hand. There was something quite attractive about it. A string through the centre of its chest made a long loop. Without really thinking about it, Andy slipped the loop around his neck and buttoned the charm inside his shirt.

He wrote back to the solicitor, thanking him and saying that he was sorry to learn of his uncle's death. But he was just being polite. He had not seen his Uncle Giles for years. He was really a great-uncle. In his day, Giles Fern had been quite famous. He had been an explorer and had visited some mysterious parts of the world. He had been in Tibet long enough to learn the language. He had disappeared in Africa for many years, apparently becoming a fully accepted member of a tribe there. There were books about his experiences. But Andy had never had much contact with him. His world of night clubs and his life with a young family were miles apart from the world of Uncle Giles. Perhaps Uncle Giles had sent him the charm because there was no one else he could think of to send it to. It was a funny thing to leave someone in your will.

It was some time before Andy began to put two and two together.

That night, he was working at a club in a nearby town. It wasn't the easiest place to be a success in but Andy was a comic who took things in his stride. He went on stage after the first two acts. Quite a lot of drinking was going on. But Andy knew his stuff and quite soon the noise died and Andy was making them laugh. One man, however, seemed to fancy himself as a comic, and he kept interrupting Andy. Andy played up to him and got the audience on his side. But the man would not stop. Andy grew annoyed and his jokes became a bit sharper. This annoyed the man and he became insulting. Andy stayed calm. The rest of the audience began to tell the interrupter to shut up. He grew angry. He stood up. He shouted that Andy's act was rubbish. He told him to get off the stage. The noise in the club grew louder and Andy, in turn, grew angry.

Then, suddenly, the man made a choking noise. He clutched his chest and fell forwards across the table. Of course, it stopped the show. When they looked at him, he was dead. He had had a heart attack.

Naturally, it depressed Andy. He told Linda about it. But, then, he did not see anything odd about the affair.

A comic's life has its ups and downs. Normally Andy would not have reacted so strongly. But he was still feeling edgy about the death at the club when his agent rang him up on the following Monday. It was about the Golden Slipper Club in Berlsdon. Andy was topping the bill there on the Friday of that week.

His agent said that there was a certain old woman in Berlsdon who had a lot of power in the town. She did not like the Golden Slipper Club. But old Mrs Wallace really hated Andy. She said she wanted the club closed because Andy's act was filthy and disgusting. The manager of the club had taken fright. He did not know if she could carry out her threat. But in any case, the agent asked, could Andy tone his act down?

Andy agreed calmly enough. But when he put the telephone down he was shaking with rage. Perhaps there were one or two crude spots in his act. But the real dirt was all in Mrs Wallace's mind. He spent two minutes silently cursing the old hag to himself. But he did clean up his act.

And when he got to Berlsdon that Friday, he found that it did not matter, anyway. Mrs Wallace had had a serious accident. It would be weeks before she would be able to cause anyone any trouble again. Andy went back to his old act that night. It was a big hit.

That was just the beginning. A club manager who cancelled Andy's act after he had driven eighty miles to get there suffered a broken ankle. Some youths who jeered at his act later had a serious smash in their car. A café owner who had a row with Andy was injured in a big fire. There were other things both large and small. It was very odd. Nothing bad ever happened to him but disaster seemed to spread around him. And it spread chiefly among the people who angered him.

It all made Andy edgy and moody. It went on for weeks. Accidents happened all round him. He brooded; he grew more and more tense. It affected his act.

Realisation came when he quarrelled with his agent. Part of Andy's bad temper stemmed from the fact that his bookings were dropping off. He went to see the agent about it. Neither of them, unfortunately, was in a pleasant humour to start with. Andy accused the agent of taking his cut and doing no work for it. The agent went so far as to say that Andy's act had always been third rate and that it had got ten times worse. Unforgivable things were said on both sides. They broke off their business relationship there and then. Andy was trembling with rage when he left the office. He could hardly get his key into the lock of his car. He was in a black mood at home. If Linda or the children tried to speak to him, he cut them short.

The truth began to dawn faintly the next day. It was just a short item in the newspaper; a fatal accident. His agent had fallen in front of a bus. He had died almost at once. He and Andy had known each other for years.

Andy went straight out of the house without saying a word to anyone. He drove down to the village near where his great-uncle had lived. He had time to think on the way down. When he started chatting to the people in the local pub, he was in control of himself. He chatted about ordinary matters at first.

Then he began, casually and tactfully, to ask questions about Giles Fern. You could feel the sudden chill in the air.

They were careful in their answers – almost afraid. He had been a strange man, they agreed. People did not see much of him.

'They kept out of his way,' one, apparently less cautious than the rest, told Andy.

'Oh?' he asked. 'Why?'

'Didn't like to run the risk of offending him,' the man said. 'Could be a bit dangerous.'

After that, neither he nor anyone else would say much more. But it was enough. Andy drove thoughtfully home. He knew then what kind of power the charm possessed.

Why did he not throw it away? Perhaps he thought he could control it. Perhaps he thought he saw some advantage in keeping it. Maybe he thought of all the years that his uncle had lived. Did the charm possess the power of giving long life as well? Anyway, he was still wearing it when he got home.

There he walked into his final quarrel. Linda had been simmering under his black moods and silences for days. When he walked out on them without a word, it brought matters to a head.

She was so fierce that he, too, flared up at once. She went for him savagely and he responded in the same way. It was the worst quarrel they had ever had in their married life. She was sure that he had been away to see another woman.

A small thing brought it to a halt. She remembered that she had to pick up the children from school. She was already late. With an angry word, she slammed out of the house, leaving him blind with anger.

It only took moments for that anger to be replaced by cold terror. But by that time she had started the car and was on her way. He went straight after her. He knew what the charm could do.

Linda had two miles to go to the motorway and about a mile and a half to drive along it. She was still angry. She drove fast at first and even faster when she was on the motorway. It was when she came to turn off for the school that she knew something was wrong with the car. It began to swing from one traffic lane to another. The steering had gone. When she put her foot down she found that the brakes had gone, too. In that dreadful moment she was sure she was going to die.

Andy drove like a maniac, his mind racing, but she was well ahead. He knew that the charm protected him. If he could get to Linda and be with her, it would protect both of them. But there were things about the charm that he did not know. It could not protect him against himself. He cornered too fast and crashed violently into a lamp standard.

He struck his head and died instantly. The car caught fire. By the time they got his body out, it was burned beyond recognition. So was the charm. Its power was dead.

On the motorway Linda found her throat too dry to scream. Death seemed as close as her own skin. Then, miraculously, the steering righted itself. The brakes came back. She controlled the car and, still trembling, drove to the school and picked up the children. Then she drove home to the terrible news.

THE STORY

1 Right at the beginning of the story is Andy Winter's family a happy or an unhappy one? What makes you think so?
2 Who probably owned the charm before Giles Fern? Can you make a guess?
3 The charm took all sorts of revenge on people who offended Andy. Was it right in what it did? What do you feel about it?
4 What does an agent do? Do you know? Can you find out? How does an agent get paid?
5 Andy went down to the village where Giles Fern had

lived. Why were the people there not eager to talk about the old man?

6 What did Andy expect to happen after his quarrel with Linda?

7 Why did she drive so fast along the motorway?

8 How did Linda manage to get her car under control again?

YOUR OWN WRITING

1 How did Giles Fern get the charm? What had he done to earn it? How did it protect him? Write his story.

2 Write out the quarrel between Andy and his agent in the form of a short play. There are some hints of the things they said in the story. You can add others of your own.

3 Write in the form of a short play the conversation Andy's agent had with the manager of the Golden Slipper Club in Berlsdon.

4 A distant relative who has travelled in strange places sends you a small bottle to keep for him. But you drink some of the liquid it contains. This gives you some kind of unusual power. Is it good or evil? What is this power and what do you use it for? Write the story.

The Tramp

I quite often take the track by Cope's Farm up to the moor. On the top, as the slope flattens out, you come to an old stone quarry with a rough road leading away from it. He was sitting hunched on a rock by the road, staring at the ruined old hut back in the quarry.

He looked very odd. He wore something like a boiler suit made of pinkish-silver plastic. It had no buttons or zips and it covered his hands and feet as well. His arms were wrapped round his body, as if he was cold. He had very short hair, he was pale and he looked the picture of misery.

I've never seen such an expression of hopelessness on anyone's face before. He stared right through me at first. Then he realised that I was there and gave a start. His expression changed to one of fear and he stood up, holding out his hands as if to protect himself.

'Nice day,' I said. It wasn't, but I felt I had to say something to calm him down. He mumbled a reply which I didn't understand. But I nodded and smiled and walked past. To tell the truth, he seemed so weird that I felt a bit scared at being alone with him up there on the empty moor. But he came after me and I stopped and turned. He spoke. I caught the word 'angry', and I wondered for a very uncomfortable moment whether he was going to attack me. Then I saw that he was pointing to his open mouth and that he had really said that he was hungry. Luckily, with my sweet tooth, I had part of a bar of chocolate in my pocket.

I shoved this at him, still smiling to show that I meant him no harm. He took it, looked at it suspiciously, sniffed it and finally peeled back the wrapper and licked it. Then he smiled, too, tore off the rest of the wrapper and put the whole chunk in his mouth.

I backed away, watching him. But he was busy eating and I left him standing there. I did turn round once or twice but he wasn't following. He was walking back to the quarry. The last time I looked back, he was just going into the ruined hut.

What would you have done? Talked to him? Found out where he came from? I could hardly understand a word he said. Would you have reported him to the police? Or made inquiries about escaped lunatics?

I did nothing. My wife died five years ago. I live quietly and manage for myself. When you're old and alone, you can't stand fuss and trouble. I didn't want to be the centre of an inquiry. Besides, I was sorry for the chap. If he had escaped from somewhere, he probably had his reasons. I wasn't going to do anything to put him back where he came from, wherever that was.

The second time I saw him he looked just like any other tramp. That was the next day. He came to my back door. He was wearing dark grey trousers, very worn old boots, an overcoat with only one button and a very battered hat with holes in it. I still couldn't make out one-tenth of what he was saying but I gave him a mug of tea, a good thick sandwich and fifty pence and sent him on his way.

He was in the district for seven or eight months. Of course, there was talk about him. Mrs Cope up at

Cope's Farm had given him the overcoat and the boots. He must have got the trousers and his jacket and the hat off Bill Slater's scarecrow. Bill Slater, when he found out, said that he was welcome to them. People were sorry for him, you see. He was young and thin and pale, and it was difficult to make out what he was saying. He seemed so helpless.

Mrs Dale down in the village wanted him to chop some wood for her as payment for the food she gave him. He gaped at her as if he'd never seen an axe or wood before, and even when she showed him how to do it, he made a mess of the job. Of course, that might just have been his way of dodging work. People went on helping him along. They thought of him as a poor feeble soul who was a bit weak in the head.

He wasn't. Perhaps I'm the only one he really opened up to. Perhaps he even told me the truth. But I'll swear he was just as bright as any of us.

He wandered about all over the place but he kept coming back up the lane in front of my house, that leads up to the quarry and the hut. He used to stop sometimes, and as I got to understand him better we started to talk. One day when I had given him a mug of tea he surprised me by asking me if I would have liked to live a thousand years ago.

'Not much,' I said, to humour him. 'There'd have been a lot of dirt and disease. None of our modern comforts.'

'Things would be difficult,' he said, giving me a strange look. 'For one thing, you wouldn't be able to speak the language. A language can change a great deal in a thousand years. Your clothes wouldn't be right and your money wouldn't be any good. The food would be quite different and there'd be a lot of things you wouldn't understand – like the sort of work people did.'

'I suppose you're right,' I said. At that time I was still thinking of him as being not quite right in the head. It seemed to me that if I had been born a thousand years ago, I would have fitted in quite well. So I couldn't see the point of his remarks. It was only later that they made more sense to me.

By that time we were all calling him 'Daft Harry' or 'that tramp', and 'Harry' to his face. His real name was Harun Ryve. And he said he had travelled back in time for nearly a thousand years.

He'd been a kind of criminal – nothing serious, he said. In his world criminals had a choice. They could either take their punishment or undergo an experiment. For instance, they might be made to test a new piece of space equipment or try out a new cure for a disease. After years of research, the scientists of his world thought they had discovered time travel. They wanted a human guinea pig to try it out. They had offered that kind of choice to Harun. It seemed preferable to the punishment, so he agreed.

He talked about time tunnels. You can't set out to travel in time from simply anywhere. According to Harun, you must go through a kind of gateway. Then you can travel along one of these tunnels to another gateway. He had come through into the ruined hut in the old stone quarry.

He had come in a transporter. That was a sort of cage of wire and metal plates and special crystals which encloses the time traveller. It had needed an enormous source of power to start it off.

Because everything was so new and untried, he said, the trip was risky. Too risky. He had travelled back to our time to find that he couldn't return to his own. He wasn't a scientist; he was only the guinea pig. He had no way of knowing what had gone wrong. Even if he could have spotted the fault, he wouldn't have had the knowledge to put it right.

He told me all this on various occasions when he stopped at the house. Then he didn't call any more.

I got news of him from time to time, though I certainly didn't discuss his story with anyone. People would have thought I was as daft as he was. I even felt quite silly when I went up to the quarry to have a look in the old hut.

There was a contraption there made of wires and metal plates with blocks of what looked like quartz stuck on in places. But what did it prove? It could have been something to do with the quarry, though the place had been closed down for years. More likely someone had been tinkering with a new kind of aerial or some other invention, found it didn't work and dumped it up there.

He stayed in the district. I was told that he earned some money from fruit and potato picking but he lived mostly by cadging what he could. With the money he earned he bought himself another overcoat from Oxfam. That made him look just respectable enough to be allowed into the library in Fordham, the nearest town.

I've been there recently to chat with the librarian – very casually, of course. But I did find out that Harry read a lot of unusual books in there – technical and scientific stuff – that sort of thing.

And there are other facts. Not too long ago a local factory specialising in high-level electronic engineering was burgled. And about a month ago, the Fordham newspaper had a headline about terrorists. A quantity of explosives and detonators had been stolen. During this time I often saw Harry in the lane outside my house which leads to Cope's Farm and the old quarry.

The blast up there, late one Thursday night, brought the police and the fire brigade. The explosion had knocked down some rocks and destroyed the old hut. There was no trace of the person who had set it off – and what was there to damage? I didn't join the crowd who went up to have a look the next day. And I didn't inquire about the contraption. I wasn't going to risk stirring up awkward questions for myself. I didn't visit the quarry until all interest in the place had died down.

The contraption wasn't there. But neither was the hut. What remained of it had been carted off when they cleared up after the explosion. They had wired off the entrance and put up a notice about trespassers. The contraption had probably gone with the rest of the rubbish. There may be no connection, but as far as I can discover, Daft Harry hasn't been seen since, either.

Still – imagine for one second that he was who he said he was. Harun Ryve – if he really existed – had done a fantastic thing. Knowing very little about it to begin with, he had studied and planned and taken a chance. By sheer luck and guesswork, he had solved his problem and got himself back where he came from. Those explosives might just have been the source of power that he needed.

And what would have happened then? The people in his time wouldn't have left it like that. They'd know the problems of time travel and because of Harun's test trip they'd know how to solve them. So they'd want to try again, wouldn't they? And they wouldn't run any unnecessary risks. They'd repeat Harun's trip exactly.

I don't think they'd come and announce themselves to us. Think of the uproar you would cause if you said you were a time traveller. There would be press and TV interviews, lie detectors and medical tests. You'd be mobbed.

To avoid all that, you'd do precisely what Harun had done. Just melt into the landscape.

I'm saying this because of something funny that happened a couple of days ago. I was looking out of the window, waiting for my breakfast kettle to boil. Two tramps came down the lane from the direction of Cope's Farm. Neither of them was Daft Harry, though they were dressed like him in dark trousers, battered hats and worn boots. One wore a brown overcoat just like the one Harry had bought from Oxfam. The other had an overcoat which could have been the one Harry got from Mrs Cope.

I thought about them all day. I saw them again in the evening, walking back towards the quarry. I haven't seen them since.

No one else seems to have noticed them except Tiny Benson, who works on the road. He saw them going towards Fordham. He spoke to them but they mumbled a few words he couldn't catch and didn't stop.

It may seem like nothing to you. But Daft Harry's tale stays in my mind. And I know that, from now on, every time I see a tramp I shall wonder.

THE STORY

1 How was the man in the quarry dressed when the story-teller saw him first?
2 What did he ask the story-teller for?
3 Where did the tramp's trousers and his battered hat come from?
4 How did he manage when he tried to chop some wood?
5 What did he say his name was? What did people call him?
6 Where had he come from?
7 What did he say he very much wanted to do?
8 What did the story-teller find in the hut in the quarry?
9 Why do you think the tramp bought a better overcoat from Oxfam?
10 What brought the police and the fire brigade to the old quarry?
11 What might have happened to the tramp?
12 Where might the two new tramps have come from?

YOUR OWN WRITING

1 In a cave you and a friend find a strange kind of machine. You both get inside and set it off by accident. It takes you on a trip in time. Where do you find yourselves? Is it interesting or frightening? Do you get back safely? Write the story.
2 A man or a woman loses his or her memory. This person is in a strange town without any money. Write the sort of conversation he or she might have with the first person he or she meets.
3 What sort of place might Harun Ryve live in, if he lived a thousand years in the future? How would people travel about? What would they eat? How would they earn money? Write about what you imagine it would be like.